Thinking and Acting Like an **Eclectic School Counselor**

For Ginny. . . .

       My Companion,

       My Friend,

       My Wife,

       My Love.

RICHARD D. PARSONS

Thinking
and Acting
Like an
Eclectic
School
Counselor

CORWIN
A SAGE Company

For information:

Corwin
A SAGE Company
2455 Teller Road
Thousand Oaks, California 91320
(800) 233-9936
Fax: (800) 417-2466
www.corwinpress.com

SAGE Ltd.
1 Oliver's Yard
55 City Road
London EC1Y 1SP
United Kingdom

SAGE India Pvt. Ltd.
B 1/I 1 Mohan Cooperative
 Industrial Area
Mathura Road, New Delhi 110 044
India

SAGE Asia-Pacific Pte. Ltd.
33 Pekin Street #02-01
Far East Square
Singapore 048763

Printed in the United States of America.

Library of Congress Cataloging-in-Publication Data

Parsons, Richard D.
Thinking and acting like an eclectic school counselor/Richard D. Parsons.
    p. cm.
Includes bibliographical references and index.
ISBN 978-1-4129-6646-7 (cloth)
ISBN 978-1-4129-6647-4 (pbk.)
    1. Educational counseling. 2. Student counselors. I. Title.

LB1027.5.P3198 2009
371.4—dc22   2009019901

This book is printed on acid-free paper.

09   10   11   12   13   10 9 8 7 6 5 4 3 2 1

Acquisitions Editor:	Arnis Burvikovs
Associate Editor:	Desirée A. Bartlett
Production Editor:	Eric Garner
Copy Editor:	Gretchen Treadwell
Typesetter:	C&M Digitals (P) Ltd.
Proofreader:	Carole Quandt
Indexer:	Judy Hunt
Cover Designer:	Michael Dubowe

Contents

Preface

*School Counseling From
an Integrative Model of Change*

It may be said that school counselors, by nature of necessity, are pragmatic practitioners. It is not unusual to find school counselors employing a variety of strategies and approaches to their work with children, less concerned about theoretical purity and more interested in efficacy and positive outcomes. However, an eclectic approach to counseling is not without support or precedent. Eclecticism has been associated with a pragmatic selection of a combination of theoretical application, and integration of any number of therapy techniques in hope of more comprehensive and functional outcomes.

Often, counselors engaging in such an eclectic approach to school counseling have done so by simply gathering numerous approaches and techniques without any subscription to a theory to bind such strategies into a coherent model. Such "technical eclecticism" often appears as a random cookbook approach to counseling our students. The current text describes one model to facilitate the theoretical integration of an eclectic approach to school counseling, and avoid the cookbook approach most often associated with eclecticism. This approach, while allowing for multiple intervention strategies and techniques, integrates this mixture by way of a cohesive model or theoretical framework. It is assumed that such an integrated approach to eclectic practice will result in more functional results. The model presented within this book is the transtheoretical model of change (Prochaska & DiClemente, 2002).

The transtheoretical model of change (TTM) is not a theory of counseling, but rather it represents an empirically derived, sequential model of general change in multiple stages. TTM provides an integrative structure to counseling practice that will serve as an effective orienting framework for school counselors' employment of multiple, varied approaches to engaging their students. TTM provides an empirically based alternative to a single theoretical approach to school counseling.

While having a better understanding of such an integrative model is valuable, understanding "theory" is insufficient. It is in the translation of this model into practice that a school counselor accrues the real benefits. The practicing school counselor must translate theory into specific, action-oriented steps to help them discern relevant student information, and then formulate and implement effective intervention strategies.

Thinking and Acting Like an Eclectic School Counselor addresses this need to help counselors translate theory into practice by learning to first think like the experts, and then *act* accordingly. The unique value of *Thinking and Acting Like an Eclectic School Counselor* is that it goes beyond the presentation of a theory and assists the reader to step into that theory, embrace it as an organizational framework and then, and most importantly, employ it to guide procedural thinking when confronted with student information.

TEXT FORMAT AND CHAPTER STRUCTURE

The book will be organized around the following parts. In Part I, the reader is introduced to a reflective practitioner model of school counseling (Chapter 1) and the fundamentals of a transtheoretical model of change (Chapter 2). With these as foundations, Part II expands on both the constructs and strategies found within the transtheoretical model of change. As will be discussed in the chapters to follow, TTM provides the framework for technical eclecticism by describing the demonstrated stages people go through in their journey of change (Chapter 3), along with specific processes that have been empirically demonstrated for use by those engaged in change, both in and outside of counseling (Chapter 4). Perhaps the most unique and useful value of TTM is that it provides the counselor with a framework for integrating stage and processes into a framework for knowing the right things to do (processes) at the right times to do them (stages). Chapter 5 offers a look at the ways school counselors can integrate these stages and processes into their counseling as they move their students to the desired outcome.

The final section of the book, Part III, invites the reader to "observe" the thinking of school counselors employing a transtheoretical model of change (Chapter 6) as it guides decisions both in session (reflection "in" practice) and between session (reflection "on" practice). The final chapter (Chapter 7) moves the reader from passively observing this reflective process to actually stepping into the case material and employing a cognitive framework to guide his or her own reflection on the case material being presented.

Research suggests that procedural knowledge—that is, the process of knowing what to do when the client does this or that—is acquired as the result of practice accompanied by feedback. Practice and feedback will be central to this text. Case illustrations (case presentations with analyses of counselor actions and the decision-making processes underlying them) along with guided practice activities will be employed as "teaching tools" throughout the text.

As with all texts of this nature, this book is but a beginning. For school counselors embracing the value and efficacy of a cognitive framework to guide their reflections "on" and "in" their practice, additional training, supervision, and professional development is a must. Hopefully, *Thinking and Acting Like an Eclectic School Counselor* provides a good springboard to that end.

—RDP

Acknowledgments

As with each of the books in this series, while I have been credited with the authorship of this text, many others have significantly contributed to the formation and shaping of my thoughts into the text you hold in your hands. First, I want to thank Arnis Burvikovs at Corwin for encouraging me to pursue this book series. I would like to acknowledge the support and encouragement I have received from my colleagues at West Chester University, and I sincerely appreciate the hard work and editorial support provided me by my graduate assistant, Erica Morrison, as well as the fine work of Gretchen Treadwell. Finally, I would like to publicly thank my wife, Ginny, not only for her professional insights but also for ongoing affirmation and support.

—RDP

Corwin gratefully acknowledges the contributions of the following individuals:

Sheri Bauman, Associate Professor
Program Director, School Counseling
University of Arizona
Tucson, AZ

Stuart F. Chen-Hayes, Program Coordinator
Counselor Education and School Counseling
Lehman College, City University of New York
Bronx, NY

Gloria Avolio DePaul, School Counselor
School District of Hillsborough County
Tampa, FL

Deborah A. Hardy, Chairperson of School Counseling Department
Irvington High School
Irvington, NY

Joyce Stout, Elementary School Counselor
Redondo Beach Unified School District
Redondo Beach, CA

Robert Walrath, Interim Associate Professor in Education and
Counseling
Rivier College
Nashua, NH

About the Author

Richard D. Parsons, PhD, is a full professor in the Department of Counseling and Educational Psychology at West Chester University in Eastern Pennsylvania. Dr. Parsons has over thirty-two years of university teaching in counselor preparation programs. Prior to his university teaching, Dr. Parsons spent nine years as a school counselor in an inner-city high school. Dr. Parsons has been the recipient of many awards and honors, including the Pennsylvania Counselor of the Year award.

© 2008 John Shetron

Dr. Parsons has authored or coauthored over eighty professional articles and books. His most recent books include the texts: *Counseling Strategies That Work! Evidenced-Based for School Counselors* (2006), *The School Counselor as Consultant* (2004), *Teacher as Reflective Practitioner and Action Researcher* (2001), *Educational Psychology* (2001), *The Ethics of Professional Practice* (2000), *Counseling Strategies and Intervention Techniques* (1994), and *The Skills of Helping* (1995). In addition to these texts, Dr. Parsons has authored or coauthored three seminal works in the area of psycho-educational consultation, *Mental Health Consultation in the Schools* (1993), *Developing Consultation Skills* (1985), and *The Skilled Consultant* (1995).

Dr. Parsons has a private practice and serves as a consultant to educational institutions and mental health service organizations throughout the tri-state area. Dr. Parsons has served as a national consultant to the Council of Independent Colleges in Washington, DC, providing institutions of higher education with assistance in the areas of program development, student support services, pedagogical innovation and assessment procedures.

Introduction to Book Series

Transforming Theory Into Practice

There was a time—at least this is what I've been told—when school counselors were called upon to calm the child who lost his lunch, intervene with two middle school students who were "name-calling," and provide guidance to a senior considering college options. Now, I know these tasks are still on school counselors' "things-to-do lists," but a brief review of any one typical day in the life of a school counselor will suggest that these were the good old days!

You do not need the research or statistics on divorce rates, violence, drug use, sexual abuse, etc. to "know" that our society and our children are in crises. Each of the multitude of referrals you receive provides you with abundant evidence of this crisis.

It is not just the increased number of children seeking your assistance that is the issue—it is the increased severity and complexity of problems with which they present. The problems addressed by today's school counselor certainly include "name calling" and teasing, but sadly, in today's society, that form of interaction can quickly escalate to violence involving deadly weapons. Perhaps you still have the child or two who is upset about misplaced lunches—or homework, or jackets—but it is also not unusual to find the upset is grounded in the anticipated abuse that will be received when his or her parent finds out.

School children with significant depression, debilitating anxieties, energy-draining obsessions, damaged self-concepts, and self-destructive behaviors can be found in any school and in any counselor's office throughout our land. Responding to these children in ways that facilitate their development and foster their growth through education is a daunting task for today's school counselor. It is a task that demands a high degree of knowledge, skill, and competency. It is a task that demands effective, efficient translation of theory and research into practice.

The current series, *Transforming Theory Into Practice*, provides school counselors practical guides to gathering and processing client data, developing case conceptualizations, and formulating and implementing specific treatment plans. Each book in the series emphasizes skill development and, as such, each book provides extensive case illustrations and guided-practice exercises in order to move the reader from simply "knowing" to "doing."

The expanding needs of our children, along with the demands for increased accountability in our profession, require that each of us continue to sharpen our knowledge and skills as helping professionals. It is the hope that the books presented within this series, *Transforming Theory Into Practice*, facilitate your own professional development and support you in your valued work of counseling our children.

Part I

The Transtheoretical Model of Change

An Integrative Model to Guide Reflection

School counselors understand that theory is the foundation for effective practice. However, theory, while intellectually interesting, remains just that—"interesting"—until it is translated into practice. To be successful in practice, a school counselor needs to use theory as an operative framework to guide the processes of gathering student information, discerning what is important from what is not, and knowing what needs to be done to move the student from the "what is" to the "what is desired."

The current book presents an integrated model of counseling with principles, constructs, concepts, and techniques that cut across, or transcend, the traditional boundaries of school counseling theories. The model presented within this text provides both the rationale and the structure for the school counselor to be truly eclectic in the selection of techniques and interventions. Chapter 2 provides an overview to this transtheoretical model of change (TTM) (Prochaska & DiClemente, 2002). While describing the fundamental concepts and constructs of TTM, the focus of the chapter and those that follow is on demonstrating the value of this model as a guide to the school counselor's reflective practice. One specific value of TTM is that it affords the school counselor the opportunity to be "eclectic" in intervention strategies and techniques within the context of an empirically supported, integrated, and coherent model of change.

However, prior to presenting the transtheoretical model of change, the reader is introduced to fundamentals of reflective practice (Chapter 1) and the role and value of theory in guiding that practice.

The School Counselor as Reflective Practitioner

1

"I don't care. I really don't. School is a drag and I don't care if I ever go to college."

—Lindsey, seventeen years old[1]

School counselors reading the above quote will be neither surprised nor shocked by the apparent apathy and lack of academic motivations suggested by Lindsey's comment. The challenge for the school counselor working with Lindsey is to find ways to identify the issues underlying the comment, and process data to help direct the creation of strategies for facilitating this student's academic achievement.

While trained to be good listeners, school counselors understand that listening is but the vehicle to understanding, and that understanding is the base from which we formulate our helping strategies. The effective school counselor is one who not only knows how to invite student disclosure, but is able to *reflect* on those disclosures in ways that guide his or her own decisions at any one moment within the counseling dynamic. It is this process of reflection that serves as the focus of the current chapter.

UNDERSTANDING STUDENT DISCLOSURES

Lindsey's declaration of "noninterest" is actually an invitation to the counselor to engage in a process of reflection in an attempt to understand this student's disclosures. This reflective process is one of discernment. It is a process through which the school counselor discerns what is important from what is not, understands the "what is" as contrasted to what is "hoped for," and develops connections to guide the student to this desired outcome.

For example, the counselor sitting with Lindsey may look for the clues, the signals, and the information that would help discern the degree of disenfranchisement the student is experiencing. Is this merely a reaction to a bad day or series of days, or does her statement give evidence of a damaged sense of self-efficacy? Perhaps the student is responding to some upheaval at home or a fear of failure or fear of success. Being able to answer these and other such questions is essential if the school counselor is to effectively intervene with this student.

The effective school counselor certainly listens to a student's story, but does so with a discerning ear in search of meaning. The counselor reflects on the data presented as well as the data needed, and it is this reflection that guides the planning and decision making that the counselor employs within and between sessions.

COUNSELOR REFLECTIONS GUIDING PRACTICE DECISIONS

The counselor's ability to reflect on his or her counseling has been identified as an essential component to effective practice (Nelson & Neufeldt, 1998). This reflection provides the counselor the means to make sense of all the data presented by a student and to connect those data with a counselor response and intervention, both at the macrolevel of case conceptualization and treatment planning and at the microlevel of moment-to-moment interaction that occurs within a session.

Reflection at the Macrolevel: Case Conceptualization

It is clear that not all student information is of equal value or importance to the process and outcome of the counseling. The effective school counselor reflects on the student's disclosures and formulates these data into a coherent, yet tentative, conceptualization of what is, what is desired, and how to move from "A" to "B."

For example, consider the situation of a student who is failing all his classes and presents as unmotivated. Perhaps the school counselor has worked with numerous students who present as "nonmotivated" and, as a result, have failing grades. While the problem is labeled with the same term, "nonmotivated," the cause for this lack of motivation is idiosyncratic to that student and thus the intervention employed must similarly be shaped in response to the uniqueness of that individual. The effective school counselor reflects upon the data at his or her disposal to shape the best intervention possible for any one student at any one time. This process of reflection effectively links the student's presenting problem to an intervention plan.

The following is a condensed view of just such a reflective case-conceptualization process. The client in this case is a fourteen-year-old Latino student, Raul, whose health education teacher wrote in the referral:

> *I am concerned about Raul. He is a recent transfer and I think I'm seeing some unusual behaviors. Raul stays in the shower following class for an excessive amount of time. He is the last to exit the locker room and has been late to his next class a couple of times. When I spoke with him about this, he became upset and told me he has to be sure to really wash so that he doesn't catch anything. I am concerned about him and would like you to see him.*

Reading and reflecting on this referral, Mrs. Jacobs, the school counselor, began to hypothesize that Raul may be exhibiting some obsessive compulsive tendencies and felt that if that were the case, she would want to know if he was in treatment or in need of a referral. Entering her session with this hypothesis, Mrs. Jacobs invited Raul to share his concerns about "catching things" and asked for detailed descriptions of his washing behavior. While she recognized she was not trained to diagnose such a condition, her thirteen years of experience, along with her training as a licensed professional counselor, has helped her to recognize certain characteristics associated with obsessions and compulsions. She used questions, clarifications, and confrontation to test her hypothesis, gathering details that would provide evidence of the characteristics of obsessions and compulsions.

As she reflected on this first encounter with Raul, she was mindful of the fact that this apparently bright, articulate youth was able to discuss his shower behavior and tardiness with a sense of calm and confidence. When challenged upon his concern about catching something, he appeared a bit coy and reframed the statement to suggest, "I just don't want to go to class all sweaty." Raul's style of response as well as the specific nature of his responses made Mrs. Jacobs question her initial hypothesis. Raul gave evidence of functioning without excessive concern or anxiety in his others classes, at lunch, or even at home where he apparently enjoyed playing with his two dogs, and expressed no concerns about "catching something."

As Raul described why he took so long in the post-gym shower, Mrs. Jacobs began to feel that his behavior was less evidence of an obsessive concern or compulsion and more of a strategy to delay exiting the shower while the other boys remained in the locker room. This observation led Mrs. Jacobs to wonder if the issue was one of some anxiety around his sexual development, extreme modesty, or perhaps his desire to simply avoid the teasing often targeted to new students. Armed with these reflections "on" her session, Mrs. Jacobs consulted with Mr. Abbot, the referring gym teacher, and together they decided that it seemed that Raul's behavior was a strategy used to avoid peer teasing and locker room "play." However, since this was merely their best guess of what was happening, Mrs. Jacobs and Mr. Abbot decided to test this hypothesis that the behavior was in response to peer teasing. It was decided that Mr. Abbot would remain in the locker room during the entire period while the students were dressing, following the gym class. The expectation was that his presence would reduce the possibility of teasing and thus expedite Raul's exit from the shower and locker room.

This planning and reflection practice is not a static, one-time process—rather, it refers to the thinking that takes place following a session or an encounter that allows the counselor to review what he or she did, what was anticipated would happen, and what in fact happened. From the initial meeting through the ending of any one "contract," the effective school counselor must gather and analyze case information, formulate new hypotheses, and develop and implement intervention decisions (Tillett, 1996). Thus, in the case of Raul, Mrs. Jacobs would certainly follow-up to assess the effectiveness of the intervention. Assuming that the intervention was successful, she may still decide to sit with Raul in order to review his social skills and his ability to respond to peer teasing with strategies other than avoidance.

Reflection at the Microlevel: Reflection "in" Process

While it is essential to use student data to develop case conceptualization and intervention plans, school counselors know that counseling is a dynamic process and cannot be staged in nice linear steps. School counselors appreciate that while they may be prepared with a well-thought plan and a well-stocked "intervention toolbox," these cannot simply be applied in a one-size-fits-all manner. The subtleties of each relationship, the unique characteristics of both participants—counselor and student—and the context of time and place, all contribute to the need for counselors to fine-tune and adjust these plans and strategies, often during the moments of interaction.

Counseling as a reflective process is one in which the counselor is simultaneously involved in design and implementation of action, "[. . .] while at the same time remaining detached enough to observe and feel the action that is occurring, and to respond" (Tremmel, 1993, p. 436). Consider the simple example of offering a tissue to a tearful student. What is the intent of such a gesture? While such a gesture appears perhaps caring and helpful, might it signal that tears are not allowed? Could offering the tissue highlight and thus sensitize a student who feels somewhat embarrassed by the tears? Are these the purpose of the activity?

The reflective counselor knows what he or she expected to achieve by this gesture and will rapidly process the student's reactions, contrasting it to what was expected, and adjusts accordingly. Therefore, the counselor who provides the tissue as invitation to share feelings may note the student's dismissal of that invitation and in turn simply state, "Ginny, you seem upset. Would you like to tell me what's going on?" Or, perhaps the counselor offers the tissues as a simple physical comfort, but notes that the client becomes embarrassed by the recognition of the apparent upset. Under these conditions, the counselor may simply lower the box and place it on the table, redirecting the student with the comment, "Ginny, I'm glad you are here. Have a seat (pointing to a chair) and make yourself comfortable."

These are not actions that can be prescribed or even anticipated. These are actions that illustrate the school counselor's ability to rapidly process the data being presented, contrast these data to what was "hoped for" or "expected," and then respond in ways that move the student to the desired outcome. This is the essence of reflective practice, a practice facilitated through the use of a counseling theory or operative model.

COUNSELING THEORY ESSENTIAL
TO REFLECTION AND EFFECTIVE PRACTICE

Most of us can follow directions to assemble a toy or build a simple structure. Opening the package we usually look for the directions for quick and easy assembly. The instruction sheets often identify all the parts included, the tools required, and even the steps to take (pictures help!). Even simple "problems" like putting a puzzle together, while not providing step-by-step instructions, make it easier by providing a picture of the finished product on the box top. Knowing the parts and having a concept of how they go together certainly makes assembly that much easier.

While many who work in a problem-solving capacity are presented with problems that are structured with linear steps leading to solutions, this is not true in the world of the school counselor. We in the counseling field are presented with situations that often have no clear beginning, ending, nor certainly predictable and linear steps toward resolution.

The upset students standing in our doorways come neither with easily identified parts nor clear step-by-step instructions. Our attending and questioning skills allow us to quickly open our "student package." However—unlike most projects that have clearly marked parts—our student provides many pieces, many items, and many points of contact that come flowing out into our session, all without the benefit of a parts list or assembly instruction. Which parts are important and which are redundant or unnecessary? Where does one start? What comes next? How do we put "a" to "b"? These are questions typically answered in the instructions provided by manufacturers but are clearly absent when the "project" is helping a student navigate his or her life crisis.

Reflecting on what the student has shared and how he or she shares it—all in the context of the complexity of the human experience, and within a specific time and place of the encounter—requires some guide, some format, or some structure, or else it will be simply overwhelming. If only one had the picture on the box or the detailed instructions of where to start and how to proceed!

While there is no one picture nor set of detailed instructions to guide us with our counseling, the utilization of a counseling theory as an organizational framework will help the counselor organize the data, make conceptual connections, find themes, and provide purposeful linkages to goal and interventions. So, prior to making any meaningful reflections and procedural decisions, the effective school counselor needs a framework—a schema— to serve as a rough template to help make sense of the data being gathered. Without such an orienting framework or theory, we truly can become "directionless creatures bombarded with literally hundreds of impressions and pieces of information in a single session" (Procaska & Norcross, 1994, p. 3). As introduced earlier, one effective model to guide the school counselor's reflective practice is the transtheoretical model of change (TTM).

THE TRANSTHEORETICAL MODEL OF CHANGE: A VALUABLE ORGANIZATIONAL FRAMEWORK GUIDING ECLECTIC PRACTICE

Transtheoretical model of change is not a new theory of counseling, but rather an empirically derived, multistage, sequential model of change. A unique value of TTM is that it provides school counselors the ability to not only know "what" to do to assist their students, but also "when" to do it.

TTM provides a model of change that will allow the school counselor to identify where a student may be on a continuum of change as well as the strategies to employ to facilitate continued movement along that continuum. TTM serves as a guide for the school counselor to know which of the many interventions available will be most efficacious at any one point in this change process.

Prior to presenting and illustrating the specific strategies and intervention techniques employed by school counselors with this eclectic, TTM-orienting framework (Part II), we will present the fundamental philosophy and core principles underlying this model (Chapter 2).

SUMMARY

Understanding Student Disclosures

- Listening to student disclosure and attempting to make meaning of those disclosures requires a school counselor to employ a model, a guide, or an orienting framework that places these disclosures into some meaningful context.

Counselor Reflections Guiding Practice

- The counselor's ability to reflect on his or her counseling has been identified as an essential component to effective practice.
- Reflection provides the counselor the means to make sense of all the data presented by a student and to connect those data with a counselor response and interventions.

Counseling Theory Essential to Reflection and Effective Practice

- Counselors work with ill-structured problems; that is, the problems addressed by counselors lack linear steps leading to solutions.
- A counselor's theory, model, or orienting framework provides the "structure" needed to begin to understand the large amount of information gathered in counseling and use that understanding to formulate effective intervention plans.

(Continued)

(Continued)

**Transtheoretical Model of Change:
A Valuable Organizational Framework**

- The transtheoretical model of change (TTM) is not a new theory of counseling, but rather an empirically derived, multistage, sequential model of general change.
- TTM helps school counselors identify where a student may be on a continuum of change and what to do to facilitate movement along that continuum.

NOTE

1. All client names and reference materials reflect composite cases and not a single actual student. All names and identifying information have been modified to insure anonymity.

The Fundamental Principles of the Transtheoretical Model   **2**

School counselors, by inclination or necessity, tend to be pragmatic. Faced with a student in crisis, school counselors tend to worry less about theoretical purity and more about effectiveness of outcome. As such, many school counselors lay claim to being eclectic in their approaches to school counseling.

Counselors gifted with a multitude of intervention strategies are prepared to be flexible and adaptable when confronted, daily, by the unique challenges presented to them. However, technical eclecticism—that is, the use of varied approaches and strategies without subscription to any particular theory or counseling model—can result in the school counselor approaching each encounter without a coherent guiding framework and thus employ interventions in a random, cookbook, hit-or-miss fashion.

For the school counselor valuing technical eclecticism, the use of a coherent orienting framework and theoretical model to guide practice decisions is essential. Such consistency in practice can be gained by embracing a model of counseling that provides theoretical integration while allowing technical eclecticism. One such eclectic model is the transtheoretical model of change (Prochaska & DiClemente, 2002).

TTM articulates principles that are applicable across theoretical boundaries (Prochaska & Velicer, 1997). These principles, discussed as follows, provide the orientation framework to guide school counselors in both their selection and timing of specific intervention strategies to employ within any one student interaction.

CHANGE AS A COMPLEX PROCESS

TTM posits that behavior change is so complex that no single theoretical approach could possibility address all of the complex forces that either facilitate or inhibit change. The fundamental assumption underlying TTM is that the elemental factors for the process of change cut across all specific theoretical approaches to counseling (Prochaska & Norcross, 1994). As a model supporting technical eclecticism, TTM draws on concepts as diverse as those found in the work of Freud as well as those posited by B. F. Skinner. As will be discussed, there is a role for techniques such as art therapy and psychodrama alongside contingency management and cognitive reframing.

As a theory of change, TTM is not without foundation. Research has demonstrated that there are specific factors and processes of change that are operative in all circumstances of change, including what occurs in and out of the formal counseling dynamic (Prochaska & Norcross, 1994). Emerging from this research is the perspective that change is a stage-based process.

CHANGE AS A STAGED-BASED PROCESS

Change unfolds in stable, sequential stages (Prochaska & Velicer, 1997; Reed, Velicer, Prochaska, Rossi, Marcus, 1997). This concept of change as following predictable, sequential stages serves as a central organizing construct of the TTM.

Counselors operating from a this model see changes in behavior progress gradually from the point where the individual is uninterested, unaware, or unwilling to make a change (precontemplation), to a position where he or she considers the need and value of change (contemplation), and only then decides and prepares to make a change.

Perhaps, over the past year, you have engaged in a personal growth "project." Maybe you have taken on a project of losing some weight. If you reflect on your own journey of change, you may discover that there was a time, perhaps eighteen months ago, when this project would have been of value, but truthfully, you were simply unaware that you had gained a few pounds and would benefit from some diet and exercise. Maybe it was a picture of you at the beach, or the experience of attempting to fit into your favorite fall outfit, that increased your awareness of the added pounds. With this new awareness, you may have made a mental contract to do something about this weight issue. You know, perhaps you mentally committed to forgoing desserts or getting up early each morning to jog. But there is a good chance that you didn't get around to either of those strategies right away. The stage theory of change would see your journey as one that was predictable and, in fact, effective and successful. Even though you had yet to engage in activities that would directly result in weight loss, such as dieting or jogging, the increased awareness and the mental commitment were steps or stages that were both needed and were, in fact, productive changes. With the renewed commitment, a plan will soon follow and, with that plan, the implementation of the action desired.

Too often, we view the change as effective when the final goal, for example losing weight, has been achieved. Such an orientation can lead to a sense of frustration, even despondency, when reaching the end goal is delayed and such a delay is viewed as failure.

School counselors employing TTM as an orienting framework approach change as a progression. Thus, even when the end state has yet to be achieved, behavioral change could still be well on its way. A student who begins to understand that a problem exists—and commits to doing something, someday—is exhibiting significant change, just as is the student who actively engages in a remedial process and succeeds at accomplishing his or her goal. The counselor employing a TTM orientation understands the various stages of change (see Table 2.1) and sees any progression as significant. This was certainly the case with Virginia, a bright, yet under-achieving, eleventh-grade high school student.

Table 2.1   Stages of Change

Stage	Description	Illustration
Precontemplation	Individual has no intent to change behavior in the near future.	Student comes to the office at the "request" of another. Typically, student has no clue as to why he or she is there.
Contemplation	Individual, while aware of the possible benefit of change, may be ambivalent and procrastinate.	Student can "own" his or her need to get serious and study more, but fails to engage in activities that would result in this increased study behavior.
Preparation	Individual intends to progress to action and may have taken small steps.	Student has actually investigated the availability of tutoring or thought about friends with whom he or she could study.
Action	Individual has made overt, perceptible lifestyle modifications.	Student has now attended a tutoring session and has worked with a peer preparing for the exam.
Maintenance	Individual works to prevent relapse and consolidate gains.	Student has committed to meet monthly with a study group and will go back to the tutor to review the midterm exams.

| Case Illustration 2.1 | Virginia: Change Is More Than an "End State" |

Virginia came to the counselor's office having been identified by her teachers as a student in danger of failing for the year. In the initial session, Virginia made it clear that she felt that there really wasn't any problem and that she had it "under control." Virginia was quick (and insistent) in noting that she would pull it together, just like she "always did in the past." The student, at this stage of the change process, was truly unaware of the existence of the real problem or the need to do anything to remedy the situation. At this point in the interaction, attempting to engage the student in specific steps to improve her grades would have fallen on deaf ears and proved ineffective. Rather than targeting the problem of failing grades, the counselor employing TTM as an orienting framework recognized that the problem to be addressed was the student's lack of awareness. In this situation, the interventions needed were not those targeting improved study habits or work productivity, but those targeting the increase in her level of awareness and ownership of the existence of a problem.

In working with this student, the counselor placed her ideas of referring Virginia to the afterschool study group on the back burner and instead turned her attention to discussing and analyzing previous semesters with this one, in hopes of helping Virginia discern what may be different and thus more threatening about the current situation. With this as the focus, the counselor was able to move Virginia from her initial perspective that everything was "under control" to her at least now stating a willingness to look at everything that she had to do in her classes and the amount of time remaining until the end of the marking period.

For some school counselors, the inability to engage Virginia in strategies aimed at immediately improving her grades may have been seen as a "failure." However, for those counselors working with a TTM-orienting framework, even Virginia's willingness to consider that this may be different than previous semesters would be viewed as meaningful movement along the continuum of change.

Counselors operating from a TTM-orienting framework understand that genuine, determined action is only taken once the student considers the need and value of change (contemplation), and then commits to making that change (commitment). Further, the research supporting TTM demonstrates that relapses are almost inevitable. School counselors employing TTM as an orienting framework embrace setbacks and relapses as part of the process of working toward lifelong change. Thus, the counselor working with Virginia understands that even though she engaged in a number of strategies to improve her grades and, as her report card shows, was successful in passing all of her courses, that Virginia may need a "booster" or "follow-up." These follow-up contacts would be geared to reduce the risk of setback or relapse, and in this case, may take the form of developing strategies to help insure Virginia's continued engagement in these remedial procedures and reduce the chances of her returning to previous unproductive behaviors. With TTM, relapses or setbacks are not perceived as failures but rather as data to be reviewed, analyzed, and employed to modify the action and steps currently employed.

Starting at Various Points Along the Continuum

Since change is progressive, the school counselor employing a transtheoretical model assumes that not all of the students entering counseling are at the same stage of change. Some students may be at the beginning stage and truly unaware of the need and value of such change, whereas others may have been considering change for quite a while, or may have even engaged in activities targeting such change. As such, understanding where the student is along the process of change is essential to developing those strategies to facilitate movement toward the desired end point.

Counselors with TTM schema also understand that while stage theory is presented as a linear sequencing of steps towards a goal, in practice, students often exhibit a spiraling or cycling back and forth across these stages as they move toward their desired end point, a point to be discussed in detail in Part II.

PROCESSES PROMOTING CHANGE

Throughout the preceding discussion, emphasis has been placed on knowing which stage the student currently occupies. The implication is that with this knowledge, the school counselor would be able to engage specific processes to facilitate the student's movement through to the next stage of change. But what processes are to be used?

TTM posits to a large degree that the change occurring during counseling could be attributed to ten empirically derived processes of change (Prochaska, Velicer, DiClemente, & Fava, 1988). The ten processes that have received the most empirical support include five classified as *experiential processes* used primarily for the early stage transitions, and five labeled *behavioral processes* used primarily for later stage transitions. Table 2.2 provides a listing of those processes, along with a brief description and illustration of each.

Table 2.2   Processes Promoting Change

Focus (Experiential or Behavioral)	Process of Change	Description	Illustration
Experiential Processes of Change	Consciousness Raising	Increasing awareness about the causes, consequences, and cures for a particular problem behavior.	When confronted, student says everything is okay with his current grades, yet the grades clearly illustrate he is failing and in danger of not graduating.
	Self-Liberation	Acceptance of personal responsibility, commitment, and power.	Student who was thrown out of the basketball game admits that he "lost it" when his opponent began "trash talking," and as a result, he hurt his team.
	Social Liberation	Increasing social opportunities.	Counselor has instituted a "buddy system" assigning students who are very popular to serve as guides and buddies to facilitate social inclusion of new students. Or, salad bars are incorporated in the cafeteria as a way to promote health and dieting for students at risk.

Focus (Experiential or Behavioral)	Process of Change	Description	Illustration
	Dramatic Relief	Increasing emotional experiences, followed by reduced affect if appropriate action can be taken.	Student is able to express her feelings of guilt surrounding the accidental death of a friend after engaging in an expressive, art-therapy activity. Or, one finds relief from repressed anger by engaging in a role play.
	Environmental Reevaluation	Affective and cognitive assessments of how the presence or absence of a personal habit affects one's social environment.	Student, as a result of empathy training, begins to understand the negative impact his aggressive attitude and behavior has on others, and subsequently, how the behavior leads to his own social isolation.
	Self-Reevaluation	Combination of both cognitive and affective assessments of one's self-image with and without a particular unhealthy habit.	Student comes to understand the fact that his own self-talk supporting his self-concept of being rejectable results in behavior (e.g., failing to make eye contact, head down, social withdrawal) that makes this self-concept self-fulfilling.

(Continued)

Table 2.2 (Continued)

Focus (Experiential or Behavioral)	Process of Change	Description	Illustration
Behavioral Processes of Change	Stimulus Control	Removing cues for unhealthy habits and adding prompts for healthier alternatives.	Counselors post "motivational posters" to highlight celebrities promoting the value of "study," "cooperation," "'goal setting," etc. Or, a decision is made to remove soda and candy vending machines from campus as a way of reducing sugar intake.
	Helping Relationships	Combination of caring, trust, openness, and acceptance as well as support for the healthy behavior change.	Student finds the counselor to be a safe, trusting, caring individual with whom he can share his most intimate concerns and be open to therapeutic feedback.
	Counterconditioning	Learning healthier behaviors that can substitute for problem behaviors.	Student with test anxiety is taught relaxation techniques. Or, the student susceptible to peer pressure is taught assertive strategies. Or, the obese student is helped with identifying and employing replacement foods for those that are detrimental.

Focus (Experiential or Behavioral)	Process of Change	Description	Illustration
	Reinforcement Management	Providing consequences for taking steps in a particular direction.	Counselor helps the student establish a plan for increasing study time, using "video game playing time" as contingent on engaging in thirty minutes of studying.
	Self-Liberation	Believing that one can change along with the commitment and recommitment to act on that belief.	Student develops a "contract" with his parents stating that when he gets honors, they will allow him his license to drive a car. The contract serves as a public commitment to both the goal and the action needed to achieve the goal.

The school counselor operating from a TTM-orienting framework believes that a comprehensive set of change processes should be employed and not be restricted to the two or three typically offered by most theories of counseling. As such, it is not unusual to find the school counselor with a TTM-orienting framework to employ each of the strategies presented in Table 2.2. However, the school counselor does not engage in indiscriminate or random use of these strategies, but rather employs TTM as an integrative model for such technical eclecticism, pointing to not only the "what" (processes) but also the "when" (stages).

INTEGRATING PROCESSES AND STAGES

Prochaska and Velicer (1997) argue that specific process and principles of change need to be applied to specific stages if progress is to occur. At each of the stages of change, different types of interventions or processes are appropriate to move the person to the next stage (Prochaska, Redding, & Evers, 2002, p. 104). With this as an orienting framework, school counselors understand that interventions should be individualized and matched to students' readiness for change. Such tailoring of intervention to the unique stage of change reduces resistance, stress, and the time needed to implement the change. Stage-matched interventions can allow all of the students, even those unsure of why they were sent to the counselor's office or those unclear about the benefits of changing, to participate in the change process.

A more detailed discussion of the relationship between these processes and stages of change will be presented in Part II; meanwhile, Table 2.3 provides a brief overview of the relationship of these processes of change to the stages of change.

Table 2.3　Integrating Stages and Processes of Change

Precontemplation	Contemplation	Preparation	Action	Maintenance
Consciousness raising (observation, confrontation, interpretation, data collection). Dramatic relief (venting, catharsis, crises intervention).	Self-reevaluation (of behavior on self and others). Consciousness raising.	Self-liberation strategies (goal setting, force-field analyses, scaling, shaping, increasing self-efficacy).	Therapy specific strategies (contingency management, counter-conditioning, stimulus control, helping relationships).	Managing the environment to increase support, reduce and control negative influences (creating supports, routines, structures, reminders that assist maintenance of new behavior).

SUMMARY

Transtheoretical Model of Change (TTM)

- This model is an empirically derived, multistage, sequential model of general change.
- It provides an integrative, eclectic perspective to articulate the predictive, sequential steps of behavioral change.
- TTM articulates principles that are applicable across theoretical boundaries.

Change as a Complex Process

- The fundamental assumption underlying TTM is that the factors that are elemental to the process of change cut across all specific theoretical approaches to counseling.
- TTM draws on concepts and strategies as diverse as those found in the work of Freud to those posited by B. F. Skinner.

Change as a Stage-Based Process

- TTM posits change as following predictable, sequential stages.
- The sequence of change progresses through the stages of precontemplation, contemplation, preparation, action, and maintenance.
- Change occurs at each stage and not merely at an end point of final goal attainment.
- Movement through stages is often spiraling, opposed to fixed, linear progression.

Processes Promoting Change

- People engage in covert or overt activities with the intent of altering their thinking, feelings, behaviors, or even relationships.
- TTM posits that, to a large degree, the change occurring during counseling could be attributed to ten empirically derived separate processes, including five classified as *experiential processes* used primarily for the early stage transitions, and five labeled *behavioral processes* used primarily in later stages.
- Specific processes and principles of change need to be applied to specific stages if progress is to occur.

Part II

Integrating Stages and Processes of Change

As noted in Part I, the transtheoretical model of change posits that change in behavior is rarely a discrete, signal event. For most people, change occurs gradually through predictive stages of development, and with identifiable processes facilitating that change. The chapters in Part II detail the constructs embraced by counselors operating with a transtheoretical model of change along with the specific interventions employed by school counselors as they facilitate the movement of their students to healthier, more effective behavior.

Chapter 3 provides a detailed look at the stages of change along with the unique opportunities and challenges presented by each. Chapter 4 describes the empirically supported processes that can be employed by the school counselor in the efforts to facilitate change, and Chapter 5 demonstrates the need, value, and processes of integrating stage and process as a guide to the selection and application of eclectic interventions.

The information presented in Part II will remain simply that, information, unless the constructs are embraced as a basis for the school counselor's reflective practice. As such, the case material presented in both Part II, and later in Part III, offers the reader the opportunity to see the specific concepts and constructs of a transtheoretical model of change used as guides to reflective practice. It is in using TTM as the orienting framework guiding reflective practice that the real value will be obtained.

The Stages
of Change

3

School counselors operating from a transtheoretical model of change
approach their work believing that change unfolds in stable, sequential
stages. Further, school counselors working from an eclectic framework
believe that knowing the nature of each stage, along with the anticipated
sequence, allows them to employ specific strategies to facilitate progression
to the next stage in the change sequence. TTM provides the school counselor
with the orienting framework needed to guide reflective practice and the
decisions and actions employed at any one point in the counseling dynamic.

The current chapter describes the nature of each stage of the change
process, the reality of the spiraling nature of change, and the specific
implication for the school counselor.

DESCRIPTION OF STAGES OF CHANGE

Precontemplation

Sitting in a school counselor's office, one will undoubtedly see the
presence of numerous students who have been "sent" to the office by a
teacher, an administrator, or even a parent. Inviting these students to
engage in a counseling relationship, with a question as simple as "What
can I do for you?" often elicits a blank stare or an intolerable level of
silence. Many of these referred students come to the counselor's office
truly not knowing why they are there. Others, while "knowing," clearly
fail to own the need or value of being there.

It is not unusual to find that our students identify the issue as not their
problem but the problem of the person (teacher, administrator, parent)
making the referral. For these students, a counselor's attempt to engage in
remedial steps or any plan of action to rectify the situation will prove
ineffective, often meeting with student resistance. That certainly was the case
for John, the fifth-grade student engaged with Ms. Federico, his counselor.

Ms. F: Good morning, John. Come on in.

John: Hi (handing her a note).

Ms. F: What's this?

John: Mr. McKane sent me down. It's the note he told me to give you.

Ms. F: Hmm (not looking at the note). I will look at this in a second, but maybe you could tell me what's going on?

John: I don't know.

Ms. F: Well, would you tell me what happened that caused Mr. McKane to send you to the office?

John: Nothing. I was just standing talking to Robert before the bell rang. I don't know? He wrote something down.

Ms. F: Okay, let me look (reading the note). Mr. McKane is saying you were disrespectful?

John: I don't know what he's talking about. I was just trying to talk to Robert before homeroom started and he told me to sit down, so I said to Robert, "I'll catch you later" and then Mr. McKane freaked out. He's got some kind of problem.

A student, like John, operating at the precontemplation stage lacks the insight into the existence of a personal problem and clearly fails to see the benefit of changing. Counselors such as Ms. Federico, while attempting to discuss the need and or value of making change, will be met with resistance.

Ms. F: Well, there seems to be some difference in opinion here. Apparently Mr. McKane feels you were disrespectful and yet you clearly don't believe you were.

John: Yeah. He's always on my case. He doesn't like me.

Ms. F: Do you think it may be worthwhile for you to try to talk to Mr. McKane and ask him what it is that perhaps he would like you to do?

John: Why? I didn't do anything.

Ms. F: Well, I guess I was thinking that maybe by you asking him what it is you could do differently, you would show him that you aren't disrespectful and are willing to try to fix the situation.

John: There's nothing to fix. I am telling you I didn't do anything. He's the one with the problem.

John's resistance to Ms. Federico's recommendations is not unexpected, given the fact that he is in the precontemplation stage of change and truly fails to see and/or embrace the existence of his own problematic behavior or the potential consequences of his behavior (Scholl, 2002). Counselors who fail to recognize the placement of this student along the continuum of change may jump into the process of recommending problem-solving steps only to find that the student actively resists by protesting that he or she did not do anything, or passively resists by giving lip service to the game plan without following through. Counselors attempting to engage students who are in the precontemplation stage in remedial action will experience resistance. These students have no real intention of changing the behavior, at least not within the foreseeable future (Scholl, 2002).

Picking up on the dialogue between Ms. Federico and John, we can see the counselor's own sense of frustration as John's resistance increases.

Ms. F: But according to Mr. McKane, he asked you twice to stop talking and for you to take your seat. Then, he writes, when you finally moved toward your seat, you said something and "rolled your eyes"?

John: Rolled my eyes? You got to be kidding. He told me to sit down and I said, "Catch you later" to Robert and sat down. Boy, he's got a problem.

Ms. F: Well, maybe it would help if you could go back after class and explain that you are sorry he thought you were being disrespectful.

John: Why should I do that? I wasn't disrespectful. He's a jerk.

Ms. F: John, I'm just wondering if you went back and showed him that you didn't intend to come across disrespectfully, if the tension may ease and you would get back into a better relationship.

John: I wasn't disrespectful. He's the one reading into it.

Ms. F: But you know, even if he is misreading into your actions, it may help for you to go back and talk to him.

John: Okay, whatever. Can I go back to class? We are having a quiz in first period.

Ms. F: Okay. Best of luck with the quiz, and think about what I said about talking to Mr. McKane.

John: Yeah, okay. Thanks.

While John's parting words implied some compliance with the recommendation, the tone and previous exchange suggests that his "okay" was giving mere lip service to the counselor and the chance of him approaching Mr. McKane was very low.

Resistance is truly the hallmark of students in this stage of change (Prochaska, DiClemente, & Norcross, 1992). School counselors working with students in this precontemplation stage need to suspend engaging in problem-solving actions and target their interventions to increasing the students' awareness and ownership of both the existence of a problem *and* the belief in their abilities to successfully resolve the problems. With an increased awareness and ownership of both the existence of a problem and the possibility that this problem can be successfully remediated, the student moves into the next stage of change, contemplation.

Contemplation

When circumstances are such that a student is unable to deny the existence of a problem, he or she will give evidence of seriously considering the problem and its implications. These students may share with the counselor that they "aren't doing so well" in their classes, or "maybe should stop smoking," or "maybe have a bit of an attitude" as evidence that they are in the contemplation stage of change. Students in the contemplation stage are aware that a problem exists and give evidence that they have given serious thought to addressing the problem (Patten, Vollman, & Thurston, 2000).

While it is encouraging to the counselor to have the student exhibit clear awareness and ownership of a problem, the counselor unfamiliar with the stages of change may become frustrated with the student's apparent lack of action and engagement in remedial steps. While students in the contemplation stage are truly aware of the problem and are seriously thinking about addressing the problem, the key phrase is "thinking about." Counselors need to remember that the student in the contemplation stage is exactly that, contemplating. These students, while talking a good game, are not really ready for immediate action, and interventions targeting such immediate action will go unheeded.

To compound the uninformed counselor's frustration, these students will not only fail to engage in corrective actions, but will often continue to engage in their problematic behaviors (Patten et al., 2000). It is not unusual for a counselor to spend an entire session having the student "see" that her failure to do homework is jeopardizing her chances to graduate, yet come to find the very next day that the student still didn't take her books home or complete her homework.

Counselors without an understanding of the stages of change may see each of these incidents as "failures," rather than recognize that the success is in the student's understanding of the problem, and initial thinking about changing, not in the actual and immediate resolution of the problem. These new experiences are not failures or setbacks, but rather additional data that may be used to help increase the student's awareness of the problem and thus reinforce the value of change.

Counselors working with a transtheoretical model of change as an operational frame of reference understand that these students are not simply placating the counselor. When they talk about wanting to change, they are in fact honestly sharing their awareness and desire. However, it is important for the counselor to understand that stating that one is aware of a problem and interested in addressing it, while a necessary condition, is not a sufficient condition for engaging in the action steps needed to resolve the problem.

Consider the situation of the student, Fred, who expressed concerns about his smoking only to be found two periods later at lunch smoking in the courtyard.

Counselor: Fred, how's it going with the smoking?

Fred: Not so good. I know we talked about it, and I really want to stop, but boy, it's tough.

Counselor: It is tough, so I hope you don't get down on yourself.

Fred: Nah. My girlfriend wants me to stop and I see all the ads about the dangers of smoking. I know I should stop.

Clearly Fred "knows" he should stop and is really thinking about it. The problem for Fred, and others, in the contemplation stage is that they really need to see both benefits of change and truly believe that change is possible. Students in the contemplation stage of change are attempting to identify the pros and cons of making change. According to TTM, this growing awareness that the advantages (i.e., the "pros") of changing outweigh the disadvantages (i.e., the "cons") shifts the "decisional balance" in favor of taking action and moves the student to the next stage of change.

Preparation

As the student moves into the preparation stage of change, he or she moves from merely thinking about doing something to actually taking small steps in the direction of change. Students in the preparation stage give evidence of intending to take action in the immediate future. The challenge at this point, however, is that some students, while motivated to change, may not really know how to proceed or experience inhibitory anxiety about their ability to change or the impact of such change. To move the student toward full action (action stage), the counselor may have to help him or her feel more confident that the intervention makes sense and that they will actually be able to follow through with the specific plan.

The counselor working with a student in the preparation stage would want to support his or her expressions of intent to change and help develop a preliminary plan of action along with some small preparatory steps he or she may be able to take. For example, consider the counselor's interaction with Kate, a fourth-grade student who is having difficulty paying attention and participating in class.

Counselor: So Kate, why the excitement? What's up?

Kate: I wanted to tell you what I did!

Counselor: Well, you certainly sound excited, so tell me.

Kate: I asked Mrs. Jacobson if I could move my seat to the front of class.

Counselor: You did?

Kate: I told my mom about talking with you and how you were going to help me do better in class. And she said why don't I try to move my seat to the front where I could pay better attention, so I did.

Counselor: Kate . . . that's super.

While Kate's decision to move to the front of the class came at the invitation of her mother, the counselor supported that small step as clear evidence of her readiness to take action. While such a step may or may not ultimately resolve the problem, it does provide evidence that the student is invested in change and is willing to employ time, energy, and talent to make that change a reality. The same would be true for the student struggling to remain alcohol and drug free. The counselor working with this student may help him progress in the change process by asking him to simply identify other guys in his group that would be interested in a "straightedge" (drug-free) contract. Even this small process of simply identifying possible social supports is a meaningful step toward becoming drug and alcohol free.

The steps typically taken by a student in the preparation stage will not be sufficient to remedy the situation. However, they are essential and sufficient for maintaining the student's interest in change and the belief that change is possible. As the student engages in these small steps and experiences success, he or she will be better positioned to engage in those actions that will result in overt behavioral change.

Action

The action stage is that which is most typically identified as "the counseling." For those unfamiliar with a transtheoretical model of change, the action stage is what needs to occur if one is to be successful in counseling a student. However, as suggested throughout the previous discussion, movement through each of the previous steps reflects real change, real progress, and real success. The action stage is simply the next stage in the process, one involving the most overt forms of behavioral change.

The student operating in the action stage has already begun to make efforts to address the issue at hand and to modify behaviors, experiences, and environments (Patten et al., 2000). A student in the action stage has committed significant resources of time and energy and has begun to receive feedback from others that this commitment to action is both obvious and clearly showing results. This was certainly true for Richard, a student who was trying to stop cutting class.

Richard: This hasn't been easy.

Counselor: Really?

Richard: Yeah. I mean sometimes I am *so* bored I just want to bolt, but I'm working on it.

Counselor: I know you are. You should be really proud. It's been three weeks and you haven't cut one class. How are you doing that?

Richard: Well, I found out that if I volunteer to work a problem at the board in math or if I come to social studies class with a question, I get more involved and the time passes quickly, so that helps.

Counselor: Fantastic. So, I guess you must be doing some homework so that you can have a good question to ask or know how to do a problem?

Richard: Yeah . . . but that's cool, since because I'm doing better my mom let me and Rod do some homework together. So I get to see him more and still do well in school.

Counselor: Richard, that's fantastic!

Richard gives clear indication of working hard and creatively finding ways to maintain his presence in class. He is certainly fully engaged in the action stage. However, the school counselor needs to be cautious. It is important for the counselor not to assume that investment in change is change. It is essential not to overlook the need to support the students in their actions as well as prepare them with the steps necessary to maintain the changes following these actions. It is through continued, successful action that a student will eventually move to a position where the problematic behavior ceases to exist and the risk that the problem behavior will return has been reduced (Velicer, Prochaska, Fava, Norman, & Redding, 1998). Movement into the final stage, maintenance, occurs when the student sees evidence of performance improvement, has a positive affective state, and receives positive social and performance feedback (Scholl, 2002).

Maintenance

As the counselor and student work through the various actions and steps, and begin to see significant reduction in the problem behavior, their attention needs to turn to processes that will secure these gains and prevent relapse of the problem behavior. While there is nothing unique about counselors employing follow-up sessions to check on their students, quite often the follow- up occurs unsystematically as time and energy allow. Counselors employing an eclectic frame of reference embrace follow-up and maintenance processes as an essential stage in the continuation of the progression of change. Just as the school counselor using a TTM frame of reference approached each of the previous steps with well thought and reasoned interventions, so too will he or she approach this final stage of maintenance.

During the maintenance stage of change, the counselor will employ strategies to facilitate the student's development of confidence and belief in the ability to maintain this new life style or behavior. Approaching maintenance as a continuous part of the change process, school counselors will systematically approach follow-up and booster sessions, and consider alternative delivery systems (e.g., classroom guidance programs, or group sessions) all geared to maintaining the gains made by their students. This is exactly what Ms. Peterson, the sixth-grade counselor did for Sean, a new transfer student who was having trouble socially fitting into his new school.

Following a successful intervention, Ms. Peterson engaged Sean in the development of a "peer ambassadors" program. The program was designed to have volunteer students serve as partners or "ambassadors" to all new students in order to help them with their adjustment to their new school. Sean took an active role in inviting students to join as "ambassadors" and he also served as an ambassador himself. Not only did his position as "ambassador coordinator" provide him the means to make and maintain his own social network, but the program held special preventive value for all those future transfer students.

CHANGE AS A NONLINEAR PROCESS

Like most books that present stage models, the stages of change have been presented as a unique, homogenous experience neatly sequenced in linear fashion with one stage leading to the next. As school counselors know, the reality when working with our students most likely reflects a different picture. Typically, progression through the stages of change is neither neat nor linear.

If we simply consider our own history of "New Year's resolutions," it may become clear that progress is marked by setbacks, restarts, and periods of relapse. In fact, research suggests that many New Year's resolvers report five or more years of consecutive pledges before maintaining the behavioral goal for at least six months (Norcross, Mrykalo, & Blagys, 2002). Rather than movement between stages of change being neatly sequenced and linear, it is more likely to appear like a vertical spiral (see Figure 3.1). That is, while progression through the stages of change is relatively forward and sequential, moving from precontemplation through to action and maintenance, there will be times of regression. Revisiting previous stages could be considered part of the normal process of change, rather than evidence of failure or occasion for feelings of hopelessness.

Figure 3.1   A Spiral Model of the Stages of Change

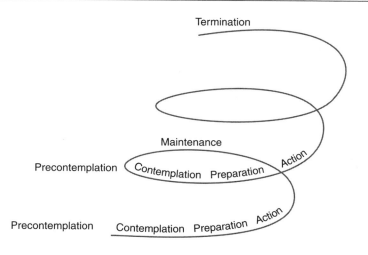

SOURCE: Taken from Prochaska, J.O. DiClemente, C.C., Norcross, J.C. (1992). In search of how people change. *American Psychologist, 47*(9), 1102–1113.

For example, a counselor may experience a student who, while having moved into a preparation stage, returns to the counselor's office once again questioning whether or not it's really worth the effort (contemplation). While such "revisiting" of a previous stage is not unexpected, it typically reflects the student's need to complete some of the specific tasks represented by the stage to which he or she has returned. Take the case of a student questioning the value of engaging in a new plan for participating in class. This student may need to revisit and analyze the pros and cons of her current behavior and contrast those to the pros and cons expected to result once change has occurred. There is a chance that the first time the counselor and student considered these pros and cons the weighting toward engaging in the new plan was not as clear-cut as originally believed. Or, perhaps, while seeing the benefits of engaging in this new plan, the student may now doubt his or her ability to be effective in engaging the plan.

These periods of relapse or regression often result in our students feeling embarrassed about their failures and may result in them feeling somewhat demoralized. The counselor who appreciates the spiraling nature of change will be able to support the student during this period of regression and, more importantly, will be able to show the student the value of the new concerns as information that will help refine or recraft the plan under consideration. By helping the student view this relapse as part of the "normal" progression of change, the counselor can help the student regain the enthusiasm and hope-filled feelings needed to reengage in the processes that will lead to the action and goal attainment desired.

STAGES AS PROSCRIPTIVE FOR SCHOOL COUNSELORS

School counselors who employ an eclectic approach such as the transtheoretical model of change as an orienting framework will find that knowledge of the student's placement along the continuum of change provides proscriptive as well as prescriptive information in regards to the specific interventions required. The school counselor working with a TTM frame of reference understands that each stage requires unique "interventions" and renders some strategies as ineffective at this point in the change process. For example, the student in the precontemplation stage, who is truly unaware of the existence of his or her problem or the need and benefit of change, will not be responsive to a counselor attempting to engage in specific action-oriented interventions. For these students, the need to feel heard and understood, and to experience a trusting relationship and working alliance with the counselor, should take precedence and serve as the primary focus of the counselor's efforts.

Once a working relationship is in place and the student has increased awareness of the current situation and the value of change, the counselor can turn attention to providing the student with the necessary corrective feedback to facilitate the student's commitment to change. This eclectic blending of interventions that promote change according to the demands with which the student presents in each stage serves as the focus of the next chapter.

SUMMARY

Stage Model

- With a stage-based model of change as their orienting framework, school counselors view "change" not simply as a singular event, such as a student passing a test, but rather see change as a process occurring over time, and thus including multiple events and experiences.
- Knowing the nature of each stage, along with anticipated sequence, allows counselors to employ specific strategies geared to facilitate progression to the next stage in the change sequence.

Stages of Change

- Precontemplation is the stage in which students do not intend to take action in the foreseeable future, usually measured as the next six months. Students may be in this stage because they are uninformed or underinformed about the consequences of their behavior. Or, they may have tried to change a number of times only to become demoralized about their ability to change.
- Contemplation is the stage in which students intend to change in the next six months. They are more aware of the pros of changing but are also acutely aware of the cons. This balance between the costs and benefits of changing can produce profound ambivalence that can keep people stuck in this stage for long periods of time.
- Preparation is the stage in which students intend to take action in the immediate future, usually measured as the next month. They have typically taken some significant action in the past year.

(Continued)

(Continued)

- Action is the stage in which students make specific, overt modifications in their behavior within the past six months.
- Maintenance is the stage in which students work to prevent relapse.

Change Is a Nonlinear Process

- While the process of change moves through identifiable stages, this progression is not always straightforward and linear.
- Movement between stages of change is more likely to appear like a vertical spiral with times of regression and revisiting of previous stages.
- The counselor who can place relapse within the "normal" progression of change can help the student regain the enthusiasm and hope-filled feelings needed to reengage in the processes that will lead to the action and goal attainment desired.

Stages as Proscriptive for School Counselors

- School counselors who employ the TTM as an orienting framework will find that knowledge of the student's placement along the continuum of change provides proscriptive and well as prescriptive information in regards to the specific interventions required.

The Processes of Change

4

School counselors employing TTM as orienting framework to guide their reflective practice use a wide variety of eclectic intervention techniques. The specific strategies are culled from ten empirically supported processes of change (see Table 4.1).

Table 4.1 Processes of Change

Process	Description
Experiential Processes	
Consciousness Raising	Conducting activities that result in increased awareness of the "what is," and the "what could be." Efforts by the individual to seek new information and to gain understanding and feedback about the problem behavior, including observations, confrontations, interpretations, and bibliotherapy.
Dramatic Relief	Experiencing the negative consequences of current problematic behavior and the relief to be gained by changing.
Self-Evaluation	Understanding that changing impacts a significant part of one's identity by contrasting the sense of self as it is prior to and after change.
Environmental Evaluation	Becoming aware of the impact that one's behavior has on others around him or her.
Self-Liberation	Believing that one can change and committing to making that change.

(Continued)

Table 4.1 (Continued)

Process	Description
Behavioral Processes	
Helping Relationships	Seeking support from others and benefiting from trusting, caring relationships.
Counterconditioning	Substituting healthier, more functional behavior for problem behaviors.
Contingency Management	Employing management of consequences (punishments and reinforcements) to encourage and support a change in behavior.
Stimulus Control	Reducing or removing cues associated with problem behavior and incorporating reminders for and cues eliciting healthier behavior.
Social Liberation	Creating policies and programs that support the healthier behavior as the norm.

Each of the processes presented in Table 4.1 represent a broad category of change "processes" encompassing multiple techniques, methods, and interventions traditionally associated with disparate theoretical orientations. The first five processes are typically used in the early stages of change, and are classified as experiential, while the last five are classified as behavior processes and are used in later stages of the change process. Each of the processes is described in detail as follows.

EXPERIENTIAL PROCESSES

The processes grouped as experiential processes target change in the way the student thinks and feels, and include strategies resulting in consciousness raising, dramatic relief, self-evaluation, environmental evaluation, and self-liberation.

Consciousness Raising

Students often present as being unaware of the existence of a problem and the need for change. For these students who are truly unaware of the depth and breadth of their problems or the possible short- or long-term consequences of a continuation of their behavior, the use of processes and strategies to increase their awareness are essential if change is to occur. Techniques and strategies such as providing information, corrective feedback, psycho-education, or even offering interpretation and providing therapeutic confrontation belong to this class of consciousness-raising processes. All of these can be used to increase a student's awareness about the negative consequences, the causes, and the cures of the problem behavior.

The strategically timed presentation of information, which may have been previously unavailable to the student, can prove to be the therapeutic confrontation necessary to move a student into a more complete aware-ness of the nature of the current situation and the role he or she has played in the creation and maintenance of the situation. For example, consider the situation where a school counselor is working with a twelfth-grade high school student whose grades have dramatically fallen, but who minimizes the long-term effects of this drop, proclaiming "this marking period really isn't that important." The counselor working with this stu-dent may choose to walk that student through the admission criteria of her college of choice, pointing out the college's emphasis on the students "consistency" in academic performance. An increased awareness of the possible negative impact that a decline in any one semester may have on her ability to gain admissions to this preferred setting may be the exact information to raise the student's understanding and ownership of the significance of this situation, and arouse her interest in engaging in reme-dial actions.

A second technique that can also significantly impact the student's level of awareness and facilitate movement along the continuum of change is the use of a timely delivered "therapeutic confrontation." Consider the following illustration of one counselor's use of confrontation to break through the student's resistance to recognizing and owning the problem at hand.

Counselor:	But, clearly the grades have dropped.
Bernadette:	Whatever. I am not sure what all the big deal is. Maybe I'm not getting all As, but so what?
Counselor:	I guess it does seem like a big deal to some people. I know your teachers were concerned and your mom and dad seem upset, but clearly you don't feel like it is a big deal?
Bernadette:	No, so what if I don't have all As. Things will be okay.
Counselor:	Bernadette, you keep saying you don't have all As and that's true, but I don't think that is your parents' or teachers' concern.
Bernadette:	What do you mean?

Counselor: Well, it's not the fact that you don't have As. The truth is that you are failing all of your classes and in jeopardy of not being promoted next year.

Bernadette: Yeah. I don't care (starting to tear).

Counselor: Bernadette, I can imagine this is pretty scary. I know you said you don't care about failing or not being promoted, but when I listen to your voice and see the tears in your eyes, it seems to me that maybe you do really care, but maybe are unsure of what to do?

Bernadette: Everyone is on my case (starting to cry and very upset).

Counselor: I'm sure it feels that way and it may seem a little hopeless, but that's why I called you down. It isn't too late and we really can do something about this.

Bernadette: What can I do? The semester is almost over!

The counselor's sensitive and well-timed presentation of information (i.e., being in danger of failure and nonpromotion), and then the confrontation, contrasting her words with her nonverbal communications, seemed effective in increasing the student's ownership of the problem and moving this resistant fifth-grade student to a point where discussion of her academic problems can begin to take place.

For some students, such direct confrontation is not possible. One strategy that has been used with students who may benefit from a less direct form of information giving or therapeutic confrontation is the use of bibliotherapy. The underlying premise is that students, when introduced to the stories of others in similar situations, will be less defensive and resistant and may identify with those within the story. For example, the child who is in denial of the pain of loss they are experiencing may be helped to become more aware of her feelings of pain and loss as a result of reading or listening to a story about another child who is grieving. The use of this strategy need not be restricted to use of printed materials. The school counselor could recommend that the student watch a particular movie and then follow-up with the student in order to discuss his or her perception and reactions to the movie's theme or specific portrayal of any one character or situation within the film. For those counselors working with younger students, the use of play activity, such as having the student draw a scene from a book read to them, can be an adjunctive activity which provides the student with an opportunity to see and embrace the nature of his or her problem.

Whatever the specific intervention strategy, be it simply supplying the student with needed information or presenting a therapeutic confrontation, the focus is on increasing the student's awareness of the issues confronting his or her own life. It is hoped that with such an increase in awareness, the student will be positioned to value the need for engaging in the counseling dynamic.

Dramatic Relief

In contrast to the information-delivering approaches employed by the counselor attempting to elevate the student's awareness and consciousness regarding the problem at hand, counselors attempting to engage the student's emotional ownership of the problem may employ processes to offer dramatic relief.

Strategies and techniques grouped under the rubric of dramatic-relief processes are those which facilitate the student's experience and expression of his or her feelings and emotions relating to the problem behavior (Patten, Vollman, & Thurston, 2000). Often this happens as a natural consequence of the student experiencing a major life event such as a loss of a relationship, the reception of a college rejection letter, a car accident, etc. These events can certainly highlight the consequences of the behavior and elevate the student's feelings about his or her current situation. Consider the following brief exchange between Thomas, a second-grade student with a somewhat explosive temper, and his counselor. The counselor had worked with Thomas on the issue of his temper, but Thomas always found ways to blame another and avoid taking responsibility for his action. Previous efforts to help Thomas take ownership for his action were less than successful.

Thomas: Hi (standing at the door sobbing).

Mr. Snyder: Thomas, come here. What's wrong?

Thomas: I did something really bad (trying to catch his breath).

Mr. Snyder: Really bad?

Thomas: My mom is going to be really angry (starting to cry).

Mr. Snyder: Thomas, maybe you could tell me what happened?

Thomas: This morning I started to yell at my mom.

Mr. Snyder: You were yelling?

Thomas: My mom told me that I wasn't going to be allowed to go the Jonathan's party this weekend because I've been mean to my baby brother.

Mr. Snyder:	So, your mom told you that you would not be able to go to your friend's party?
Thomas:	Yes, and it really made me angry. I started to yell and she told me to go to my room (starting to cry again).
Mr. Snyder:	It's okay, Thomas. Let's see if we can work this out. So, you yelled at your mom and she sent you to your room. Is that correct?
Thomas:	Yeah, but I did something really bad.
Mr. Snyder:	Could you tell me what you did?
Thomas:	I went in her bedroom and I started to throw things and I think I broke the picture frame of my grandfather when he was a little boy. She's going to kill me (crying).
Mr. Snyder:	So, you lost your temper, and as a result, broke something that was very important to your mom? I know you are afraid about how your mom will react, but I get the sense that you are feeling something else?
Thomas:	I am sorry (crying). I didn't mean to break it. I don't know why I did it. She's going to be really sad. I didn't mean to do it (crying). I really didn't. I just got really angry.
Mr. Snyder:	It sounds like when you got angry, you kind of lost control over what you were doing?
Thomas:	Yeah, I didn't mean to do that.
Mr. Snyder:	But when you are angry, you sometimes do things that make you sorry, later?
Thomas:	I don't know what to do. My mom's going to be so mad.
Mr. Snyder:	Thomas, it sounds like there may be two things that are upsetting you. First, I know you are worried about how your mom is going to react to the broken picture frame. Maybe you and I can talk with your mom together. But the second thing that seems to be upsetting you is your temper, and things you do when you are angry?
Thomas:	I wish I could stop (still upset). My mom is going to be so sad (crying).
Mr. Snyder:	Thomas, you really do sound like you wish you could stop getting so angry and losing your temper. How about if you and I start working on helping you with that?

It is clear that Thomas's initial concerns centered on the possible consequences of his action, but his tone, body language, and words spoke to the fact that he was truly engaged at the emotional level and experiencing the real negative emotional consequences of his temper outbursts. He has broken through his resistance to owning his problem, and is in the position to begin to take steps to reduce these outbursts.

In the absence of such natural events that result in such emotional experiences and dramatic relief, the counselor may turn to strategies such as storytelling, role playing, or psychodrama to engage the student at the emotional level (Velicer et al., 1998). Storytelling, for example, is a strategy that invites the student to engage at a personal, emotional level in a way that circumvents direct confrontation or conflict. Storytelling can indirectly alter the student's perception through a role identification process that is critical for dramatic relief. The counselor using this strategy engages the student by recounting a story of his or her professional experience with a student who exhibited or experienced a similar situation as the student with whom the counselor is currently working. In sharing the story, the counselor would highlight the unexpected negative consequences of that student's attitudes and/or behaviors as a way of emotionally engaging the client-student in the story. The counselor then explores the emotional reactions that the story elicits and invites the student to imagine his or her own feelings if these consequences were personally experienced. When successful, the effect of storytelling is to help the student identify that a problem exists and position the student for contemplating the need to change. Consider the following brief exchange.

Counselor: You know, Roberta, I probably should apologize because I know I'm sounding like I'm lecturing you about drinking and driving, but it is something that is really close to me.

Roberta: It's okay. I know you are just trying to help, but really, no need to worry. We are never too drunk to drive.

Counselor: I know that's what you think, and truthfully, that's what is concerning me. I mean, I had this same conversation with a student a couple years back. She was absolutely convinced that she knew when she was too drunk to drive, and as she said, she "never got that drunk." The sad part is that she did and she didn't know it. I was called to the hospital at eleven o'clock on a Saturday night, after she rammed into a car three blocks from her home.

Roberta: Was she okay?

Counselor: Well, it depends what you mean by okay. She just had a few cuts and bruises, but the car she hit had a mother and her five-year-old daughter in it and the daughter died at the scene of the accident.

Roberta: Oh, my God!

Counselor: I haven't been able to connect with her in over a year, but I know the last time I saw her, she was a mess. She dropped out of college and was not doing very well. I can't imagine what she was going through. Could you imagine how you would feel knowing that your drinking and driving resulted in the death of a child?

Hopefully, the dialogue that ensues as result of this (true) story will help to elevate the student's level of awareness of her own behavior and the risks it presents, along with the benefit of embracing the need to change.

Self-Evaluation

Self-evaluation is the process of taking a cognitive and affective assessment of the student's own self-image with and without the problem behavior (Velicer et al., 1998). The techniques included under the umbrella of self-evaluation processes facilitate the students' ability to compare and contrast their current experiences with the best-guess view of self and life after change.

Counselors attempting to facilitate a student's reevaluation focus him or her on discovering the pros and cons of initiating change. It is important for the student to identify both the payoffs and costs for both remaining as is and contrast that to the potential payoffs and real costs for making change in an identified direction. This process is geared to helping the student resolve ambivalence and conflict regarding change, and thus move the student closer to taking remedial action.

Consider the situation where an eighth-grade student, having come to grips with the reality that he could be cut from the football team because of the possibility of being placed on academic probation, commits to completing all his homework from this point on. While the student sees this homework completion strategy as a viable way to improve his grades and maintain his football eligibility, both positives, he may also identify possible costs to this plan—costs that could interfere with the plan's enactment if not recognized and addressed. As the student envisions life after this change, he "sees" that his current group of friends may make fun of him, reject him, and, in fact, if they see him going home with his books, even taunt him.

Clearly for this student, his reevaluation of his self-image following this change, while desirable, also brings with it possible costs that may impede his change and need to be addressed. The identification of both the "what is" and the "what will be" can allow the student and counselor to begin to problem solve in order to reduce possible costs of change, and reinforce the positive self-image that will result from such change. In this case, the concern about social rejection, or even social punishment, may be resolved with a step as simple as providing the student two books, one to be left at home and one at school. The simple distribution of the two books can reduce the possibility that he will be teased, taunted, or even attacked by the neighbor gang who would see his new studious self as something to be mocked.

Strategies such as employing value-clarification exercises, identifying healthy role models, and guided imagery can facilitate this self-evaluation (Velicer et al., 1998). Consider the poignant exchange that occurred between the ninth-grade counselor and a student struggling with his decision to "come out of the closet" regarding his sexual orientation. The counselor's reflective, nonjudgmental style, along with the gentle probing questions, therapeutic confrontations, and use of imagery helped this student to move closer to taking the steps toward change that he desired.

Counselor:	Rob, it is a very difficult thing to decide, but maybe it would help if we could try to imagine what your life would be like if you did decide to tell your parents and friends about being gay.
Rob:	It's hard to imagine. I mean, when I hear you say that, I almost want to throw up and go run and hide.
Counselor:	Throw up? It sounds like the image is very upsetting, very painful?
Rob:	I really don't know. I think my mom and dad will hate me. They will kick me out. I'll be all alone. But when I say that out loud, I know that's not true.
Counselor:	So, when you think about it, you are pretty clear that your parents won't hate you or kick you out?
Rob:	I know they won't.
Counselor:	Okay, but if your parents wouldn't be so rejecting, how do you see the relationship being after you told them?
Rob:	I mean, I'm sure they would be shocked, and then maybe upset, but my parents love me. I know that, and so I think they will be mostly concerned about me and how I am doing.

Counselor:	Okay, so what would you be able to tell them about how you are doing? I mean, if they knew how you have been prior to telling them, and then how you think you will feel once you have told them, what would be different?
Rob:	I don't know. I hope I could really tell them how horrible it has been, feeling like I have to hide and really feeling like something is wrong with me and hating myself.
Counselor:	So, keeping this a secret has really been hard and painful for you?
Rob:	It's getting worse and I just want them to know and show me it's okay.
Counselor:	And if I understood what you said earlier, you really believe your parents would be ultimately supportive and caring and loving once they knew, and then that would help you feel better about yourself?
Rob:	I really do. I really feel that I would feel less ashamed and just better about myself. It's not that I'm ashamed of being gay. I'm not. But I just hate feeling like I'm living a lie and not being honest with my parents.
Counselor:	So even though the discussion with your mom and dad would be difficult, you can "see" the positive long-term effect of sharing this with them in that both you and they would then be more honest and genuine?
Rob:	Yeah. But boy, thinking about doing it makes me nervous!
Counselor:	You feel nervous now, but I'm wondering, if you closed your eyes and allowed yourself to see how you would feel and act after sharing the information, what would that look like?
Rob:	That's easy (closing his eyes). I could sit at dinner and be relaxed and laugh like I used to, and be willing to hang out with my mom and dad on weekends rather than avoiding them for fear they may ask me about my "girlfriend" or "prom date." I don't know. I just see myself with lighter, you know, without a major weight on my chest . . .

The counselor's ability to guide Rob to "envisioning" life after disclosure, compared to the feelings and behavior that he is currently experiencing, helped provide this student the emotional relief necessary to increase his desire to move in the direction of disclosure. With such relief, Rob will now be positioned to work with the counselor on developing specific strategies and steps he can take to achieve that goal.

Environmental Evaluation

Often, counselors find it difficult to engage students in a remedial plan of action because they really are "okay," and perhaps even comfortable, with their own behavior and the consequences they are experiencing. These students may present in ways that suggest that they truly don't care about the problem or the situation in which they find themselves. Quite often, the student's apparent comfort and acceptance with the current situation is because he or she fails to see the impact the behavior has on others whom the student may actually care about. Counselors may find it beneficial to engage the student in an evaluation process to heighten awareness of the impact his or her behavior has on these people who are also affected. Strategies that expand the student's view of the nature of the problem, and its impact on others of significance in their lives, are identified as "environmental evaluation" processes.

The school counselor attempting to engage this process of environmental evaluation will employ techniques to get the student to see the need for change in order to avoid undesirable consequences for those significant others in his or her social environment. One strategy that may prove effective in facilitating this process of environmental evaluation is empathy training (Velicer et al., 1998).

Helping a student understand how another person may feel as a direct result of his or her behavior can facilitate the student's ownership of the significance of that behavior. The elementary school student, for example, who is helped to understand the intense feelings of isolation and sadness that a classmate may experience as a result of a comment such as, "I don't want her on our team," or the middle school student who is able to step into the experience of a student being made fun of and humiliated at lunch as a result of being poor and not having the latest in "cool fashion," may both begin to reconsider their own actions toward these students.

Empathy training can enhance empathetic feelings and understanding and increase prosocial behavior. The specific components within empathy-training approaches associated with increases in empathy include:

- Teach the student what empathy is and how to recognize different emotive states both in himself or herself and others, as well as how to respond positively to others.
- Facilitate the student's awareness of his or her own feelings and how different feelings may be associated with different situations.
- Provide experiences to help the student recognize the similarities and differences between him- or herself and another person.

Self-Liberation

Self-liberation processes address the student's belief that he or she can change. With a strong belief that efforts to change will be effective, the student will be more likely to commit to take action towards enacting that belief (Patten et al., 2000).

The school counselor targeting this process of self-liberation will employ eclectic strategies to strengthen the student's internal commitment and belief in both the value and possibility of successful change. A key objective for all strategies targeting such self-liberation is to heighten the student's belief that both the desired outcome is possible, and that he or she is capable of engaging in those activities required to be successful. This belief in the achievability of a goal, and the personal possession of skills and resources necessary to achieve that goal, has been termed self-efficacy (Bandura, 2001; Pajares & Urdan, 2006).

Students who are ready for action often need to articulate a step-by-step plan of how they will accomplish their goals. Such an articulation helps to concretize the plan, and further strengthens the commitment to change. In addition to developing a plan, the student's sense of self-efficacy or belief in the possibility of being successful, might be enhanced by engaging the student in specific skill-building activities including coaching, role play, and behavioral rehearsal. Clearly, in the following example, the plan employed, along with the supportive training by the counselor, facilitated Larry's belief in his ability to become socially assertive.

Counselor: So, you are really clear that you want to go to the prom and that you would like to ask Liz to go. So let's figure out what steps we could take to make that a little easier to do.

Larry: It would be a lot easier if I knew she'd say yes.

Counselor: Okay. So how might you go about checking that out?

Larry: I guess I could kind of "hint" at it with Kate. She's Liz's best friend, and we are on yearbook staff together.

Counselor: Super. So, how would you do that?

Larry: I don't know. We meet everyday after school to go through pictures of last year's book to see what kind of things we want to do in ours. I guess if we are looking at prom pictures, I could say something.

Counselor: Fantastic. But what do you think you might like to say? Why not role play it with me.

Larry: "Kate, look here, last year's prom pictures, their theme was 'best years of our life.' Do you know what our theme is?"

Counselor: Larry, that's super . . . really subtle. So, let's assume you start talking about your prom theme etc. What do you do next? How about if she asks you if you are going?

Larry: I guess I could say I'd like to, but not sure if the girl I want to ask would go?

Counselor: Well, the only possible problem I could see with you being so vague about who this girl might be, is that maybe Kate would think you are going to ask her?

Larry: Oh, not a chance. She and Ralph are solid and going together. But I guess I could just say I wonder if Liz would go and see how she responds.

Counselor: Cool. But let's try it. "Larry, are you thinking about going?"

Larry: "Yeah I think so. I'd like to ask Liz, but I'm not sure if she would go with me?" Boy (smiling). That makes me really nervous saying that.

Counselor: I wonder if you said, "I'd like to ask Liz but I'm not sure if she's going or maybe even has a date?" That way Kate might be able to encourage you to ask or if she thinks it's not a good idea, she can ease into it by saying something like she's not sure if Liz wants to go.

Larry: I like that. I can do that. We have a meeting today after school and I'm going to try that.

Counselor: Great. Can't wait to hear how it goes!

While the counselor is interested in Larry's prom date, she is more interested in encouraging Larry to speak up and assert himself in this and other social situations. The planning and brief role playing she employed targeted the development of Larry's sense of self-efficacy as the foundation for increasing his commitment to action.

BEHAVIORAL PROCESSES

The processes of change grouped within this category target assisting a student's development and maintenance of new, more adaptive and effective behaviors. The processes to be discussed include those that provide support by way of employing helping relationships, counterconditioning or engaging alternative ways of responding, using reinforcement and punishment as contingency management, modifying environmental triggers in the process of stimulus control, and finally, engaging social networks in support of change in a process of social liberation.

Helping Relationships

There is sufficient empirical and anecdotal evidence (Culley & Bond, 2004; Egan, 2002; Ellerman, 2001) that supports the value of a caring, unconditional valuing and genuine helping relationship. In the context of such a working alliance, students feel free to disclose and are open to corrective feedback. This, in turn, facilitates a change in the problem behavior (Patten et al., 2000). But, the positive impact of such support can be found outside of the counselor's office as well as in the one-on-one connection with the counselor. Engaging the student in social supports that are both informal, such as friends and family, and more formal, such as a buddy systems, peer groups, and counseling groups, can facilitate the student's action taken on targeting change.

A counselor working with a student who has committed to increasing her homework completion and concentrated study behaviors, for example, may connect the student with a "study buddy" or develop an afterschool study group, as ways to provide the social context and helping relationships that will support this commitment to action. Similarly, a student seeking to reduce his alcohol consumption may make an informal contract with a friend to engage in alternatives to "partying" on weekends.

Counterconditioning

While a student's current behaviors may, on face value, be ineffective and even dysfunctional, the truth is that at some fundamental level, these behaviors do serve some purpose for that student. Perhaps a student who is socially withdrawn does so because at a minimum level, it protects him or her from social rejection. Or, consider the student who fails to complete his homework and gets failing grades. Perhaps, even though failing, he is able to maintain his and others' beliefs that he could pass if only he did the homework. What happens if he does the homework and continues to fail? Refusing to do the homework works in that it prevents him from facing his feared cognitive inadequacy and the humiliation that would result if that became public.

Under these conditions, the students considering change need to find alternative, healthy ways to resolve the problem that, at minimum, also insure the same level of payoff and "protection" as the current behavior. Techniques grouped as processes of counterconditioning require the individual to learn to substitute healthy behaviors for problem behaviors (Patten et al., 2000) and include interventions such as relaxation training, systematic desensitization, assertion training, and positive self-statements (Velicer et al., 1998).

Consider the plan developed for Antonio, a third-grade student who, when encountering performance anxiety, would begin to cry and then engage in temper-tantrum behaviors. The counselor working with Antonio recognized that such temper tantrums, while accruing some negative consequences, provided momentary "relief" from the stress and anxiety being experienced. As such, the intervention developed not only targeted reducing this negative behavior, but did so while also providing a similar, or greater, sense of "relief."

Counselor:	Antonio, you are doing fantastic. You really have become a master at "stop-plop-relax" (smiling).
Antonio:	Yeah. Mrs. Haltead says it's okay for me, anytime I need, to put my head down to just do that.
Counselor:	And what is it you do when you put your head down?
Antonio:	Like you showed me. When I start to get that weird feeling in my stomach, I just say "stop," and then I plop my head down on the desk and then practice taking ten slow breaths.
Counselor:	That's super. Does it help?
Antonio:	Uh-huh. I haven't been crying and it makes me feel good.
Counselor:	Antonio, I am really proud of you and so happy this is working.
Antonio:	Mrs. Haltead is going to teach it to the class so everybody can do it, and she wants me to show them how to do it (smiling).

It is clear that this counselor has done a lot of work with Antonio prior to this point in the exchange, but using the relaxation response as a substitute for the tantrum behavior not only is more socially appropriate, it also serves the purpose of reducing the uncomfortable anxiety even better than the previous tantrum behavior.

Contingency Management

The use of positive reinforcement and contingency management to help create and sustain a student's new behaviors is not new to school counselors. Contingency management provides consequences to the student for participating in problem behavior or for following through and avoiding the problem behavior. When structured by the counselor, the use of reinforcement, even for small changes, will facilitate the student's shaping of the behavior toward its ultimate desired outcome.

It is important for counselors to remember that rewards can be extrinsic as well as intrinsic. While it is highly desirable for the counselor and student to create meaningful ways to provide the internal reward that comes with the student feeling good about achieving, being successful, and in general feeling good about him- or herself, there are times when these "natural payoffs" may not be readily available to the student and when external rewards may be needed. For the student who is unable to experience the natural payoffs for completing his homework, the counselor may help him or her to develop a plan where engaging in a highly desirable activity (e.g., playing a favorite video game) is made contingent on completion of nightly homework. Such a plan may be productive in facilitating the student's initial stages of behavior change and maintain his or her interest until more natural payoffs (e.g., improved grades, feelings of achievement) occur.

Procedures included as processes of contingency management include contingency contracts, overt and covert reinforcement, self-reward, and group recognition (Prochaska & Velicer, 1997; Velicer et al., 1998).

Stimulus Control

When a student's inappropriate behavior appears to be elicited by specific stimuli or cues, or when new, more desired behaviors seem to be supported with the presence of specific stimuli or prompts, the counselor will want to employ eclectic strategies targeting the processes of stimulus control. Stimulus control is the process in which the individual needs to remove any stimuli associated with the problem behavior and replace it with prompts to participate in healthy behaviors (Patten et al., 2000).

Restructuring one's own environment to include those stimuli, social support, or cues for healthy behavior, while reducing the stimuli, including people who have been associated with and continue to prompt problem behaviors, will help support appropriate change and reduce the risk of relapse. For example, stimulus control strategies would direct a student engaging in a weight reduction program to ask her mom to avoid having empty-calorie snacks (candy, cakes, etc.) available, replacing them with readily available fruits and cut vegetables for afternoon snacking. Similarly, the counselor working with a student attempting to stop smoking cigarettes may encourage the student to stay in the cafeteria at the end of the lunch period rather than go outside with some of the students where they are most likely to engage in smoking.

Social Liberation

It is easy, as an adult, to suggest to a teen or preteen the need to stay away from peers who seem to engage in some problematic behaviors, but for the student, the absence of an alternative social grouping makes such a decision very costly. The concept of social liberation as a process of change points to the fact that for some students, changing their social roles and engaging in new social supports will help them maintain their behavior changes. With new social environments and interactions, a student will find that the cues previously associated with old behavior will be reduced and those supporting change will be increased.

The counselor working with a student who is attempting to change his or her social behavior or increase academic performance may try to foster this student's development of a new cadre of friends, or engage the student in a specific club or group at school that embodies and values the new behavior this student is attempting to develop. Often, it may be up to the counselor to actually create such a group to support not just this student, but others experiencing similar difficulty in changing. As such, a counselor working with a young student struggling with his own sexual orientation may work toward changing school policies and even developing programs to increase the sensitivity of teachers and students toward gay students. All of these steps target the process of social liberation and support the student's efforts to change.

INTEGRATING STAGE AND PROCESS

While the strategies discussed and grouped under the specific processes of change are neither unique nor original to the transtheoretical model of change, they are empirically supported processes when used effectively—the special value of TTM is that it helps increase the effective use of these strategies by way of including the element of "timing." In simple terms, it could be stated that, *successful change appears to depend on doing the right things (processes) at the right times (stages).* This eclectic integration of stage and process as the basis for reflective practice is the hallmark of a transtheoretical model of change and serves as the focus of the next chapter (Chapter 5).

SUMMARY

Theoretical Integration and Technical Eclecticism

- Theoretical integration of multiple approaches to counseling provides strategies that will lead to more comprehensive and functional outcomes.
- TTM posits that counselors should employ a comprehensive set of change processes and not be restricted to the two or three typically offered by most theories of counseling.
- TTM identifies ten separate, empirically supported processes of change, which, when employed at specific points in the change process, will prove effective.

Experiential Processes of Change

- Consciousness Raising: Conducting activities that result in increased awareness of the "what is," and the "what could be." Efforts by the individual to seek new information and to gain understanding and feedback about the problem behavior, including observations, confrontations, interpretations, and bibliotherapy.
- Dramatic Relief: Experiencing the negative consequences of current problematic behavior and the relief to be gained by changing.
- Self-Evaluation: Understanding that changing impacts a significant part of one's identity by contrasting the sense of self as it is prior to and after change.

- Environmental Evaluation: Becoming aware of the impact that one's behavior has on others around him or her.
- Self-Liberation: Believing that one can change and committing to making that change.

Behavioral Processes of Change

- Helping Relationships: Seeking support from others and benefiting from trusting, caring relationships.
- Counterconditioning: Substituting healthier, more functional behavior for problem behaviors.
- Contingency Management: Employing management of consequences (punishments and reinforcements) to encourage and support a change in behavior.
- Stimulus Control: Reducing or removing cues associated with problem behavior and incorporating reminders for and cues eliciting healthier behavior.
- Social Liberation: Creating policies and programs that support the healthier behavior as the norm.

Matching Stage   **5**
and Process

As noted at the end of the last chapter, successful change appears to depend on doing the right things (processes) at the right times (stages). The transtheoretical model of change provides just such an integration of process and stage. School counselors employing TTM selectively employ their intervention strategies as directed by the student's stage of change, in a process that could be called stage-matched approach to interventions.

This stage-matched approach allows the school counselor to individualize interventions, in an eclectic manner, and match them to the student's readiness to change, thus reducing resistance and providing early success. For example, students who enter counseling in the earlier stages of change (i.e., precontemplation and contemplation), while on the surface may appear to be resistant and unlikely candidates for successful counseling, are more likely to experience desirable change when the counselor employs stage-appropriate processes such as consciousness raising, dramatic relief, and environmental evaluation than if the counselor attempts to immediately engage the student in actions targeting a change in the problematic behavior. Research suggests that such stage-matched interventions, which are specifically targeted at an individual's stage of change, are more effective in promoting that change (Dijkstra, van Wijck, & Groothoff, 2006; Spencer, 2006; Youngho, 2008).

Within this context, the role of the school counselor becomes one of identifying the tasks (stage related) and techniques (processes) that are required to help the student move through the stages of change toward his or her ultimate goal. Within the counseling dynamic, the focus of counselor's reflection and decisions will be on helping the student move along the continuum of change, addressing each new set of challenges found in progressive stages until the final goal is reached and maintained. To do this effectively, the school counselor will need to integrate his or her eclectic processes (techniques) with the student's stage of change.

INTEGRATING PROCESSES AND STAGES OF CHANGE

The school counselor working with a TTM frame of reference understands that not only should the interventions be tailored with respect to stage of change, but designed to promote and enable the student to accomplish the tasks presented at each stage along the continuum of change. Table 5.1 provides an overview of this integration of process and stage.

Table 5.1   Stage-Process Integration

Processes of Change	Stages of Change				
	Precontemplation	*Contemplation*	*Preparation*	*Action*	*Maintenance*
	Consciousness Raising				
	Dramatic Relief				
	Environmental Reevaluation				
		Self-Reevaluation			
		Self-Liberation			
				Contingency Management	
				Helping Relationships	
				Counterconditioning	
					Stimulus Control

As previously described (Chapter 3), students in the precontemplation stage lack understanding of the need for change and thus lack the motivation and intention to invest the resources needed to insure change. Counselors attempting to engage these students in remedial action steps will be met by resistance, since at this stage, the student truly lacks an understanding and ownership of the need and value of change. Without such an awareness of the need and benefit of change, these students will lack the motivation, or attention, necessary for engaging in corrective action and will resist the counselor's attempts to engage them in a plan of corrective action.

To be effective in moving these students toward action, the counselor needs to resist the urge to begin action planning. With students in this precontemplative stage, the school counselor needs to employ processes that result in the student's increased awareness and ownership of the problem and an increased motivation and desire to change. The effective school counselor will be alert to provide the information needed to highlight the existence of a problem and the potential personal consequences that may result.

To facilitate this movement toward awareness, the school counselor will find that providing support and employing nondirective interventions, such as strategic reflections, questions, and gentle confrontation, will be effective in moving this student along the continuum of change (Groth-Marnat, 1997). One useful technique to help elevate the student's level of awareness of the importance and value of change is motivational interviewing (Miller & Rollnick, 2002).

Motivational interviewing (Miller & Rollnick, 2002) employs cognitive dissonance (Festinger, 1957) as a way of evoking natural interest in, or motivation for, change. The school counselor employing this strategy will lead students to an awareness of a discrepancy between their behaviors and their beliefs or perceptions. For example, the student who protests that she doesn't really care about what her classmates think of her might be confronted by the reality that she has gone out of her way to be or do whatever her peers request. Or, the student who protests that he doesn't want to go to college, and therefore doesn't care about grades, may be asked to consider why it is that he has taken all academic courses as opposed to a work-study program. The challenge is not meant to be a "gotcha" type experience, but to simply present the student with the reality that there seems to be two conflicting experiences going on, and with this recognition, the student should experience a tension—a dissonance that he or she will seek to resolve. It is this arousal of dissonance, and the natural drive to remove the dissonance, that reduces the student's initial indifference to the counseling and positions the student to move into a contemplation stage of change. The following illustration demonstrates the power of cognitive dissonance as a condition facilitating awareness and ownership of the need for change.

The interaction occurred in the fourth session between the counselor, Dr. Gadaleto, and his ninth-grade student, Wally. Dr. G. had been working with Wally around issues of his apparent unsafe, sexual promiscuity. Dr. G. had been quite concerned that Wally dismissed the seriousness of his behavior and the potential negative consequences (unwanted pregnancy, contraction of STDs, etc.) as a result of his failure to either abstain or engage in safe-sex practices. We pick up the exchange following a brief "emergency bathroom break."

Dr. G: Everything okay?

Wally: Yeah, just had to go. Thanks.

Dr. G: I know I'm sounding like I'm stuck, but Wally, I am really con-
           cerned. You know I am worried that you are so sexually active
           and that you don't practice safe sex, and I'm concerned about the
           possible consequences of that behavior.

Wally: I know, but I'm okay. I mean I never . . . well you know, I don't
           stay in . . . you know . . .

Dr. G: I assume you mean your birth control technique is to withdraw
           before orgasm?

Wally: Yeah, that's it . . . and I'm really good at control, so I won't get
           anybody pregnant?

Dr. G: I know we've talked about this and you are convinced you are in
           control, because as you say, you "can feel when something is
           about to happen." But you know what? I noticed something, and
           I don't mean to embarrass you, but . . . did you see you had a
           little wet spot on your pants when you came back from the
           bathroom?

Wally: Ouch (looking down). I guess I was rushing.

Dr. G: Well, it's not so much why it happened. I guess my concern is
           that it did happen and you were not aware that it was happening.
           You know, you weren't feeling it? So I guess I wonder, how can
           you be able to be absolutely sure that you will feel any early
           exchanges of sperm when you are engaged sexually?

Wally: Huh? You mean stuff happens even when I'm not you know
           . . . getting off?

While there certainly is much more to do in this situation, the very
fact of highlighting the minor "accident" caused enough cognitive dissonance that Wally was at least now inviting the counselor to provide additional information. Such a request positions the counselor to move this
student from precontemplation to contemplation, and eventual action.

From Contemplation to Preparation

The student who is at the contemplation stage of change possesses an
awareness of the problem, but has not engaged in the steps or even committed
to the steps necessary for change to occur. Students in the contemplation stage

experience ambivalence about change, grappling with the reasons for and against changing. To move from simply thinking about doing something (contemplation) to actually engaging in some preliminary steps (preparation) to do something different, the student will need to see that the pros and cons of making a change outweigh the pros and cons of maintaining the present behavior (Scholl, 2002). Students at this point need to be helped in seeing the value of an alternative approach to their lives. One strategy that a school counselor might employ with a student at this stage of change would be to engage in a "cost benefit analysis" of change.

Cost benefit analysis helps the student assess the desirability of a change in behavior when contrasted to the status quo. For the process to be effective, the student needs to be helped in identifying all the physical, social, and psychological costs and benefits to both changing and/or maintaining the status quo. Too often, counselors try to help the student only by highlighting the costs of the current behaviors and promoting the potential benefits of change—without recognizing and discussing the fact that change involves costs and that the status quo, while costly, also provides payoffs. It is essential that all pros and cons for both—remaining as is or changing—be identified and discussed. The assumption is that with such an articulation of costs and benefits, the decisional balance will shift to engaging in the change process as opposed to maintaining the status quo. This was certainly the case for the counselor working with Raina, a tenth-grade student having some difficulty with cutting class and her "attitude" about school.

Raina: I know. I know. This is getting ridiculous. This is the second time I got caught cutting class. I know I've got to stop.

Counselor: Raina, you certainly are aware of the consequences of cutting class. I mean, you said besides having in-house suspensions, your grades are dropping and your parents are refusing to let you take your driver's test. I guess these are the "costs" or "cons" for cutting class. But, I'm wondering, what are the benefits? You know, what are the payoffs or pros for cutting?

Raina: Huh. There aren't any benefits. I'm just digging a hole.

Counselor: Well, I can't disagree that there are quite a few costs, but you know what? I have found that typically when people do things, especially when they do them repeatedly, there typically is some type of payoff for them. You know, that somehow the behavior works for them. So, I guess I'm wondering how cutting class "works" for you?

Raina: Well, I guess I'd rather be outside than sitting bored in class.

Counselor: Okay. So cutting class is less boring than being in class?

Raina: Not all the times, but sometimes.

Counselor: Okay, any other payoffs?

Raina: I can talk to my boyfriend. He's homeschooled and I call him at home.

Counselor: Okay. That's another "payoff." Anything else?

Raina: No not really. I think that's it.

Counselor: So, if I kind of put out two options and make a table of pros and cons, it would look something like this (making a table):

Option	Pros	Cons
Cut Class	More exciting to be outside.	Grades dropping.
	Speak to boyfriend on phone.	In trouble and disciplined in school.
		Not able to get driver's license.
Stay in Class	Participate in class and grades improve.	Bored.
	Parents are happier and allow driver's test.	Can't speak with boyfriend at that moment.
	Stay out of in-school suspension or discipline actions.	

Counselor: Does that sound like it? Could you add anything?

Raina: Well, a pro for staying in class is my friends want me to, and my phone bill would be less.

Counselor: That's great (adding it to original list). Anything else?

Raina: No. I think that's it.

Counselor: Well, I bet if we could figure out how to shift the pros you get for cutting class over and make them payoffs for staying in class, then maybe you would be less tempted to cut?

Raina: I'm not sure I understand.

Counselor: Well, if somehow you were never bored in class, and if by staying in class you had more or at least better opportunity to talk with your boyfriend, do you think it would be easier to stay in class and not cut?

Raina: Oh, yeah . . . sure. But how do we do that?

Counselor: Now that's a great question, and I don't have an answer off the top of my head, but I bet as you and I think and talk about it, we can come up with some pretty creative steps you could take. But before we do that, I'm wondering if there are any other costs or cons to cutting class we may have missed.

Raina: Yeah, as we were talking, I remembered my mom said if I didn't stop calling Rod during class that she would take my cell phone and restrict the times I could go see him . . . that would be a cost.

Counselor: That sounds like a pretty big cost?

Raina: Yeah, that wouldn't be very cool.

Counselor: Okay. So, it seems the more we look at the costs to cutting class, the less attractive cutting is starting to look?

Raina: Yeah, I guess . . . but I get so bored.

Counselor: Right, and that's why we also want to figure out how to increase the positives, the payoffs . . . you know, the pros for staying in class.

While the counselor has not introduced specific steps targeting increasing Raina's interest in class or ability to contact her boyfriend at more appropriate times, she has set the stage for making these steps more valuable to the student and thus increased the possibility that Raina will actually invest in these actions once this value has been identified.

There are times, however, when a student can clearly articulate the cost and benefits of change, but still appears stuck in the contemplation stage. TTM posits that in addition to modifying the decisional balance, and thus making change more desirable, the student needs to have the belief and the confidence that he or she can make and maintain the changes that are now seen as desirable. It is possible that such a student is stuck in contemplation because negative cognitions undermine the ability to move toward action. These are students with beliefs and self-talk such as: "I can't do it," "It won't work," "It would be horrible if I tried and failed," and such perceptions inhibit their movement toward the next stage of change. Counselors working with these students can promote movement by helping the students first identify, then debate and reframe these cognitive-emotive issues and develop a greater awareness of their abilities to prove successful in this change process. The counselor may find the use of cognitive therapy and rational emotive techniques (Kazantzis, Deane, Ronan, & L'Abate, 2005; Parsons, 2009b) to be particularly useful for students in this stage of change.

In addition to removing negative cognitions that may be blocking student movement toward action, the counselor would want to facilitate the student's development of a sense of self-efficacy (i.e., a realistic belief in one's ability to be successful in achieving a goal). Without such a sense of self-efficacy, the student, while desiring change, will doubt that such change is possible and therefore find him- or herself stuck in the contemplation stage. This was the experience shared by Maurice, a twelfth-grade student concerned about his "partying."

Counselor: So, if I understand, it seems really clear to you that the weekend "partying" has quite a few negatives tied to it, including the fact that you have gained weight and are not in shape for track season, that your parents have grounded you and taken away your car privileges, and that you almost got picked up for a DUI?

Maurice: Yeah, and really, it's just not fun like it was before. I mean, I like hanging out, but every weekend it's the same old thing, with the same old people.

Counselor: Maurice, you really sound like you see the limited payoff and increasing costs to continuing this partying on weekends.

Maurice: Yeah, I do. But, I don't know. I mean, all my friends seem to be doing this and I don't know, I mean what will I do on weekends? I mean, what do I do if they call me and get on my case about not going? I don't know if I can say no.

Counselor: That is pretty tough. I mean, when you get a lot of pressure to do something, especially when the pressure is coming from people you like, it is hard to say no. I guess I'm wondering if you have ever had to turn them down in the past? You know, was there a time or a situation when they were putting on the pressure, but you were able to say no?

Maurice: Well, last week I had to tell them I couldn't because I couldn't. I was grounded.

Counselor: Okay, that's good. I mean, I know you were grounded so in fact you couldn't go out, but in either case, you actually did say no. That's a good example, but I wonder, were there any other times when you weren't grounded and could physically go out, but decided not to and said no?

Maurice: Yeah, I guess. I mean, I know last year, when we had Saturday track meets, I would tell them that I was staying in and going to bed early.

Counselor: That fantastic. I mean, that is great example where you could go out, but you understood that it would "cost" you the next day, and then you decided that it was more important to be in good shape for the race than to go out and party, and you did say no thanks.

Maurice: I guess.

Counselor: Well, think about it. You didn't have your parents to blame or couldn't use being grounded as an excuse. You just made a good decision about what was best for you and you did it. So, it seems to me that on those occasions when you really understand that staying away from partying is really the best thing for you, then you do have the ability to say no.

Maurice: Yeah, you're right. And actually, I really do need to start working out. In three weeks, we begin Saturday practices. If I can remember that and get myself to run on Saturdays, I know I will be able to say no to the Friday night partying. I guess I can "just say no" (smiling).

It is clear, even from the brief exchange, that Maurice does see the benefits of saying no to this partying behavior, and now, with the guidance of his counselor, he has identified his ability to make that decision and implement it. For Maurice, the decisional balance has shifted in the direction of change and his insight into his abilities and previous experiences with saying no have strengthened his sense of self-efficacy. Helping the student, like Maurice, see the benefits of change and increasingly hold the belief that change is possible will facilitate the student's movement from contemplation to preparation.

From Preparation to Action

Students in the preparation stage give evidence of having taken small steps that are prerequisite to action leading to change. For example, the counselor working with Raina may come to learn that she has moved her seat to the front of class as a step to increase her attention and participation in class. Or, in the case of Maurice, perhaps he has asked some teammates if they would be interested in Saturday early-morning runs. These small steps indicate the students' developing commitment to change. The counselor can facilitate this progression by helping structure the plan of change so that it provides small steps, clear objectives, and a sequence of clearly achievable goals. Specific interventions may be employed at this point, including goal setting and goal-scaling activities found in solution-focus therapy (deJong & Berg, 1998; Parsons, 2009c) and behavioral shaping strategies discussed in behavior modification literature (Miltenberger, 1997; Parsons, 2009a; Spiegler & Guevremont, 2003). The intent of these processes is to ensure early successes and help the students structure the most plausible plan, given their resources, to achieve that change.

From Action to Maintenance

Students now fully entrenched in the action stage have demonstrated both a commitment to, and actual investment in, change. The review of the research suggests that the processes of reinforcement management, helping relationships, counterconditioning, and stimulus control have been identified as those most typically used with individuals at the action stage of change. While considering these processes as potentially useful, however, school counselors working with students who give evidence of owning their problems and embracing and valuing the benefits of change, need to call upon those interventions proven effective (in research or their own professional experience) for the particular type of student with the type of concern in each particular setting and context (Parsons, 2008).

As the interventions take effect and the student gives clear evidence of achieving his or her goal of change, the temptation may be to terminate the relationship as being successfully completed. However, school counselors employing a transtheoretical model of change as their orienting framework realize that the change process is not complete. Subsequent to the action stage, students enter a maintenance stage in which they demonstrate a willingness to actively continue the actions necessary for sustained change. The school counselor working with the student during this stage of change would engage the student in an education regarding relapse and assist the student in developing socially liberating strategies that will provide continued support for the changes. Engaging the student struggling with drug and alcohol issues in a twelve-step group, or helping an elementary school student with separation anxieties identify a "bus buddy," or even developing ongoing support groups for students experiencing a variety of problems ranging from social issues to academic and achievement difficulties, are all examples of socially liberating strategies targeting maintenance of change and reducing relapse.

FINAL THOUGHT: A MODEL IS JUST A MODEL

As presented in the previous chapters, the transtheoretical model of change provides an eloquent view of the process and stage of change along with the benefits of a stage-matched model of school counseling. However, as is true for all models, TTM remains simply that, a model, until it is embraced, practiced, and assimilated into the reflective practice of the school counselor. The chapters found in Part III will help move this model from the sterile presentation of theory and make it come alive as a framework guiding the eclectic counselor's reflection and decisions.

SUMMARY

Stage-Matched Counseling

- School counselors employing a transtheoretical model of change selectively employ their intervention strategies as directed by the student's stage of change, in a process that could be called stage-matched approach to interventions.
- Stage-matched approaches allow the school counselor to individualize interventions and match them to the students' readiness to change, thus reducing resistance and providing early success.

From Precontemplation to Contemplation

- School counselors working with students in the precontemplative stage of change need to employ processes that result in the student's increased awareness and ownership of the problem, and an increased motivation and desire to change.
- To facilitate this movement toward awareness, the school counselor will find that providing support and employing nondirective interventions, such as strategic reflections, questions, and gentle confrontations, will be effective in moving students along the continuum of change.
- Motivational interviewing is a strategy that could help move the student toward increased awareness and ownership over his or her problem and to begin to contemplate the value of change.

(Continued)

(Continued)

Motivational interviewing employs cognitive dissonance as a way of invoking a natural interest and motivation to change.

From Contemplation to Preparation

- Cost benefit analysis helps the student assess the desirability of a change in behavior when contrasted to the status quo. For the process to be effective, the student needs to be helped in identifying all the physical, social, and psychological costs and benefits to both changing and/or maintaining the status quo.
- When the cost benefit ratio is clearly in favor of change, the student's decisional balance will be shifted in that direction and movement toward the preparation stage will occur.
- In addition to having the decisional balance shift, the student will also need a belief in his or her ability to be successful in the change process. The creation of this self-efficacy can be facilitated by structuring activities that provide early success.

From Preparation to Action

- The counselor can facilitate this progression by helping structure the plan of change so that it provides small steps, clear objectives, and a sequence of clearly achievable goals.
- Specific interventions may be employed at this point, including goal setting and goal-scaling activities found in solution-focus therapy and behavioral shaping discussed in behavior modification literature.

From Action to Maintenance

- As the interventions take effect and the student gives clear evidence of achieving their goal of change the temptation may be to terminate the relationship as being successfully completed, but there remains one final stage—maintenance.
- Students in the maintenance stage demonstrate a willingness to actively continue the actions necessary for sustained change. The school counselor working with the student during this stage of change engages the student in an education regarding relapse and assists them in developing socially liberating strategies that will provide continued support for their changes.

Part III

TTM Guiding Reflective Practice and Eclectic Approach

A Look at the School Counselor in Action

The previous chapters introduced the principles, constructs, and strategies of a transtheoretical model of change. The real value of this model is accrued once employed as a framework guiding the school counselor's eclectic thinking, reflective practice, and decision making. But what does "thinking" like a TTM expert entail, and how is it developed?

A review of the literature identifying differences between "expert" and "novice" professionals points to the fact that those with expertise encode, organize, and use client information in ways that facilitate reasoning and problem solving much differently than those new to the profession. Rather than organizing student data into categories that are based on superficial, irrelevant cues that may not be pertinent to generating a problem solution, experts employ organizational cognitive structures—schemas that help them quickly make sense of the information that a student presents (Chi, Feltovich, & Glaser, 1981). Student data are stored in problem-relevant categories connected by underlying conceptual principles relevant to the problem solution.

In addition to employing more effective organizational cognitive structures to discern the relevant from the irrelevant, and to store these data efficiently, experts employ procedural knowledge to guide their interactions with students while in session. The effective counselor actively reflects on the information provided by the student and uses those data as guides to his or her own reactions and interventions. The effective, "expert," school counselor approaches counseling organizing the material presented by the student into "If [condition phase], then [action phase]" statements. The expert counselor knows that, "If the student presents with this, then I'll do that."

Developing the ability to employ a TTM framework guides this "If . . . , then" procedural thinking, in order to know what to do and when to do it, and leads to an increase in the school counselor's effectiveness. Developing procedural thinking requires that we move beyond simply understanding and storing concepts and constructs and begin to employ these concepts in practice. The final two chapters of this book (Chapter 6 and 7) are designed to support the development of this procedural knowledge using TTM as an eclectic framework to guide you and your reflective practice.

Chapter 6 provides an in-depth look at two school counselors in action as they address student concerns using TTM as a guiding framework. Each case provides a look into the methods and strategies employed by a counselor. However, more than an illustration of the application of TTM principles, each case also provides some insight into the counselor's procedural thinking and the utility of TTM as a guide to counselor decision making. The intent of providing a look into the counselor's thought processes while engaging with the student is that with this perspective, you may employ TTM to also process the data presented by these students and anticipate the needed responses. It is in developing that anticipation that you will have employed procedural knowledge from a TTM orientation, thus "thinking" like the expert!

In Chapter 7, you are invited to become an active participant in the processes of reflective practice. As was the case material found in Chapter 6, student data and verbatim exchange is provided, but in Chapter 7, there are a number of points in the encounter where you will be invited to stop and reflect on the data presented, and then anticipate the direction to be taken. You will then have the opportunity to see the choices made by the counselor in this situation as well as that counselor's "thinking" that guided that decision and direction. It is hoped that this vicarious engagement with the case materials, as well as the ability to contrast your thinking with that of the scripted counselor, will help you move beyond simply knowing and understanding, to now owning and doing school counseling with an eclectic perspective from a TTM orientation.

School Counselors   **6**
Reflecting "in" and
"on" Practice

The current chapter invites you to begin the process of using TTM as the filter through which to interpret student data and to direct an eclectic approach to intervention. In this chapter, two cases will be presented, each illustrating a school counselor's use of a transtheoretical model of change to guide reflective practice. As noted in the introduction to Part III, it is suggested that as you review each of the cases and observe the interaction between the student and counselor, you attempt to use your understanding of the TTM to anticipate the counselor's thinking and subsequent action.

In the first case, the school counselor illustrates her reflections starting with her review of the initial referral. Even with these preliminary data, this counselor begins to generate an initial hypothesis about what may be going on, and uses these as the springboard for her case conceptualization and treatment plan. Once engaged with the student, the counselor demonstrates her ability to be flexible and adjust to the specific needs of the student and the data being presented at any one moment in that encounter. It is her reflections during practice that allow her to adjust her interventions "in" process to help this student move from the precontemplation stage of change to the preparation stage.

The second case highlights the various strategies employed by a counselor as he helps the student develop and implement an action plan. As you read the illustration, you will become aware of the power of our natural resistance to change and the risk of relapse, along with the strategies available to TTM-oriented school counselors to guide the student toward problem resolution and maintenance of a more adaptive and functional style.

CASE 1: JEROME

Starting with the initial intake, the effective school counselor allows counseling decisions to be guided by: (1) a process of data gathering, (2) reflecting on that data, and then, (3) drawing conclusions through the use of an operative model to direct his or her actions. For the eclectic counselor employing TTM as an orienting framework, initial reflections guiding practice focus the counselor on identifying the student's placement along the continuum of change. With the belief in the need to integrate process with stage, the school counselor employing TTM seeks to gather data to not only clarify the nature of the problem, or the student's resources available for resolution, but also the degree to which the student is aware of the problem and values the need and possibility of change.

In this first case, the case of Jerome, we will "see" the counselor's reflection and practice decisions as she moves from the initial referral through to engaging the student in identifying and owning the problem, as well as committing to the change process.

Initial Referral

Jerome is a fifth-grade student who is referred to the school counselor by his science teacher, Ms. Pettigrew. Ms. Pettigrew expressed frustration with Jerome's apparent negative attitude and general lack of motivation. In the referral, she states:

> I am really frustrated with Jerome's attitude in class. He clearly doesn't care about the fact that he is failing, and every time I try to talk to him he just gives me a flip statement such as, "I don't care." I'm not sure if you can help, but he's heading down the wrong path and is going to fail science and probably fifth grade.

Reflections Prior to Meeting

As Ms. Shatz reads the referral, she immediately begins to "hypothesize" about the possible sources of Jerome's failure to do his work and his apparent negative attitude. However, as a school counselor with an eclectic perspective employing a transtheoretical model of change as an orienting framework, Ms. Shatz also begins to speculate about the degree to which Jerome owned the problem and would be open to investing his resources in a process of change.

Ms. Shatz checks Jerome's current grades and discovers that he is passing all his classes with the exception of science. Teacher comments suggest that Jerome generally completes his homework and participates in class, except, of course, science. None of the other teachers report that Jerome has a discipline problem nor presents with a negative attitude in class. Ms. Shatz begins to wonder about what is unique about science, or Ms. Pettigrew's classroom, that may be contributing to the problem. In addition, she anticipates that Jerome, being successful in his other classes, may fail to see the current situation as "his" problem, and as a result, be reluctantly entering this counseling relationship from a precontemplation stage of change.

Armed with these operating hypotheses, Ms. Shatz intends to employ processes targeting the precontemplation and contemplation stages of change (see Table 6.1). Specifically, she prepares to use fundamental relationship building skills as a way to tap Jerome's perception of the situation, while at the same time being selective in her reflections, summarization, and confrontations in order to guide him toward increased awareness and ownership of the problem at hand. The goal for this first session is to facilitate Jerome's movement from a precontemplation stage of change to contemplation and, perhaps, preparation.

Table 6.1 Stage-Process Integration

Case 1: Jerome			
	Precontemplation	*Contemplation*	*Preparation*
Process of Change	Consciousness Raising Dramatic Relief Environmental Evaluation		Self-Evaluation

Session 1: Establishing a Working Alliance

Ms. S: Good morning, Jerome. Thanks for coming down to talk with me.

Jerome: Hi (quietly sits down).

Reflection "in" Practice

Jerome appears a bit "edgy," but I'm not sure if he's angry or anxious. I wonder if this is what Ms. Pettigrew means about negative attitude?

Ms. S: How are you?

Jerome: Fine (curtly).

Ms. S: Jerome, you sound a little annoyed?

Jerome: I'm not sure why I had to see you.

Ms. S: Oh, so you are a little annoyed with me because I called you down to the office?

Jerome: No. I'm not mad at you. I know Ms. Pettigrew told you to see me. She's on my case.

Ms. S: Oh, so you are not mad at me, but are upset with Ms. Pettigrew because you believe she's on your case?

(Continued)

(Continued)

Reflection "in" Practice

Jerome sounds calm and is in control, but it is clear that he feels somewhat "victimized" by Ms. Pettigrew's referral. I think it's important to build an alliance with him so that he doesn't feel like I'm also on his case.

Ms. S: I'm sorry that you feel that way. Well, I'm not going to be on your case. I just really want to see if there is something I can do to help you with your classes.

Jerome: I'm doing okay in my classes.

Ms. S: So, you are doing well in your classes?

Jerome: All but Ms. Pettigrew's class.

Ms. S: That sounds correct. You know, we have just given out the interim reports and I saw that all of your teachers said that you were participating in class and doing your work, and generally doing well in most of your classes, except of course science, where you seem to be having some difficulties?

Jerome: I'm not having any difficulties (angrily). It's Ms. Pettigrew. I told you, she's on my case. She doesn't like me.

Ms. S: Well, I'm sorry to hear you feel that way. Would you tell me a little about your experience in science class?

Jerome: I hate that class. I wish I could drop it or get in another section. I don't know what's up with Ms. Pettigrew, but I can't do anything right in her class. She's always yelling at me and stuff.

Reflection "in" Practice

I am sure it feels like Ms. Pettigrew is always on top of him, but I know her well enough to know that's not the case. He seems comfortable with me, so I wonder if I could maybe challenge him a little regarding his role in this situation. If he will engage on that topic, it may help to raise his own level of consciousness regarding the existence of "his" problem.

Ms. S: She's always yelling at you?

Jerome: Yeah, she doesn't like me.

Ms. S: Jerome, it would help me to understand if you could tell me a little about the last time she was on your case?

Jerome: Yesterday. We were preparing to do a little lab on weight and volume, and Ridley and I were partners. So, we're getting out our equipment and Ridley is making some joke and I start laughing. Well, Ms. Pettigrew tells me to stop clowning around and says that if I can't get it together, then maybe I should go down to the principal's office. I didn't do anything, and she's hollering at me!

Ms. S: So, Ms. Pettigrew saw you laughing and thought that you were not taking the lab seriously, and therefore she told you to get focused on your assignment. Do I have it right?

Jerome: Yeah, but all the others kids are looking at me like, "Oooh, you're in trouble" kind of thing.

Ms. S: Oh, so what made it really uncomfortable for you was the fact that the other students were making fun of you? And how did you respond?

Jerome: Well, I told her I wasn't clowning around.

Ms. S: Oh, and when you told her, did she seem to understand?

Jerome: No. She sent me to the office.

Ms. S: She sent you to the office for telling her you weren't clowning around?

Jerome: Well, no. She said I yelled at her and was being disrespectful.

Ms. S: Oh. So, what started out as a little joke between you and Ridley kind of spun out of control?

Jerome: Yeah, I told you, she is always on my case.

Ms. S: Well, yes you did, and maybe that's how it felt. I'm wondering if the fact that other kids were starting to get into it, and kind of make fun of you, if that made you mad and maybe your anger came out in your tone when you tried to explain that you were not clowning around?

Jerome: Maybe.

Reflection "in" Practice

Whew! I wasn't sure he'd allow me to confront him and suggest that he contributed to the escalation. I wonder if I can shift the conversation to him and away from Ms. Pettigrew, as a way for him to take ownership of the problem, while at the same time recognizing that he is empowered to resolve it.

Ms. S: I guess that could explain the misunderstanding with Ms. Pettigrew. You know, maybe she misread your tone of voice as being annoyed at her?

(Continued)

(Continued)

Jerome: Well, I was annoyed at her, but I wasn't disrespectful.

Ms. S: Okay. So, you really didn't intend to show disrespect, but maybe the fact that you were annoyed with Ms. Pettigrew, and the other students were teasing you, made you come across really much more angry than you intended?

Jerome: Yeah, I guess.

Ms. S: You know, I'm wondering, what was it about the other kids going "oooh" that made you so angry?

Jerome: They're all thinking I'm a retard. Like I don't understand anything and don't deserve to be in this honors class.

Ms. S: So, the other kids were saying things like that to you?

Jerome: No, but they all know I'm screwin' up. Ms. Pettigrew posts our labs and projects and everybody can see I'm the worst one in the class.

Ms. S: Oh, so the class is kind of hard for you and you get embarrassed when your graded labs or projects are put up with the other kids?

Jerome: Yeah (getting upset). I hate that class.

Reflection "in" Practice

It seems like Jerome is having a little difficulty in this honors class, and when he is corrected or there is evidence that he is struggling, he gets embarrassed and upset and then blames the teacher, which results in him acting in ways that draw more negative attention to him. I wonder if I could help him see this pattern as a way of maybe turning the attention back to him, in hopes that he sees the need and value of working on this?

Ms. S: When you say you hate this class, do you mean you hate science?

Jerome: No. I like science and I always did well in it until this year.

Ms. S: Oh. So, you like the science, but you don't like the kinds of things that you have to do in this honor's class?

Jerome: No. I like the labs and stuff, but I just can't get it. I feel like a loser in there.

Ms. S: Well, I certainly can understand how that would make the class not so enjoyable. I guess that's true for me too. We really don't want to come across like we are out of it, or dumb, or like you said, a "loser," but I'm wondering, what is it that you think is making you feel that way in Ms. Pettigrew's class?

Jerome: Ms. Pettigrew is always picking on me.

Reflection "in" Practice

Well, I was hoping he was moving to the contemplation stage, but he is still disavowing ownership over the problem. I will try to set up some cognitive dissonance to see if I can get him to take some ownership.

Ms. S: I know that you said Ms. Pettigrew is picking on you, or at least correcting you, in front of the class.

Jerome: Yeah, all the time.

Ms. S: Hmm. I am wondering, do any of your other teachers ever correct you in class? You know, like if you and Ridley are goofing off?

Jerome: Yeah (smiling). Ridley's a nut.

Ms. S: Ridley does have a great sense of humor. But I am still wondering, when these other teachers correct you in class, do you feel like a loser?

Jerome: No.

Ms. S: Oh, okay. And when these other teachers correct you, do you get angry with them, and show any "attitude" toward them?

Jerome: No. I just stop messing around.

Ms. S: So, with these other teachers, you just get back to doing your work and you don't feel like a loser or get angry.

Jerome: Yeah.

Ms. S: I wonder what it is that makes you feel and act so differently when Ms. Pettigrew corrects you, like she did when you and Ridley were goofing around as you got ready for that lab?

Jerome: I don't know. I'm just frustrated in that class (getting upset). My grades stink and all the other kids seem to do better. I just feel so dumb.

Ms. S: Jerome, I'm really sorry to hear you feel so badly about yourself in that class.

Jerome: Yeah (mumbling, sadly, with head down).

Ms. S: Let me see if I get it. In your other classes, you sometimes goof around and the teacher may correct you, but you don't get mad or feel embarrassed because you are doing well in that class and feel good about yourself. Is that right?

Jerome: Yeah.

(Continued)

(Continued)

Reflection "in" Practice

It sounds like Jerome is lacking self-efficacy in science class. He apparently is not only doubting his ability in that class, but is also seeing his difficulty as evidence of being incompetent. He seems open to reframing the situation so that he can take more ownership and stop placing the blame on the teacher.

Ms. S: You know, Jerome, you really have helped me see something.

Jerome: I have (looking up)?

Ms. S: Yep. I mean, if I put my scientist hat on right now, I would make the following hypothesis. Do you know what that is . . . a hypothesis?

Jerome: Yeah. We had that in class. It's a best guess or something like that.

Ms. S: Fantastic. Well, here's my "best guess." I wonder if all of sudden you started getting really good grades on your tests and projects, and then all of your papers that were hanging on the board were as good or better than most of the others students in class, if then, when Ms. Pettigrew corrected you—you know, like for cracking up with Ridley—if then you would respond to her like you respond to all your other teachers? You know, you would just get back to work and not be angry?

Jerome: Maybe.

Ms. S: Well, if that is the case, then that's super news, because it means we don't have try to figure out how to change your class or change Ms. Pettigrew. We just need to help you do better in that class and I think we can do that!

Jerome: I don't know what I can do. This is a hard class and she may still be on my case even if I do better.

Reflection "in" Practice

Jerome is clearly in transition to the contemplation stage. He's not fully entrenched in contemplation, still assigning the problem to Ms. Pettigrew, but the fact that he is "owning" the degree to which his poor performance may be contributing to his reactions in her class says that he is moving in the right direction. Plus, the disclosure that "this class is hard" is clear evidence of owning at least part of the problem. If I am to get him into a preparation stage, I need to use encouragement and support to have him start to believe that a solution is possible.

Ms. S: Boy, you are right on! I mean, you could do really well and Ms. Pettigrew may still be on your case, as you say, but you know what? We won't know if Ms. Pettigrew will still be on your case until we test this out.

Jerome: Yeah, I guess.

Ms. S: But Jerome, I thought we decided that the real issue was how you felt about yourself in that class and not really whether or not Ms. Pettigrew was correcting you.

Jerome: I guess.

Ms. S: Well, remember, you said that when other teachers correct you in classes where you are doing well and feel good about yourself, then their correcting you doesn't seem to be so upsetting.

Jerome: Uh-huh.

Ms. S: So, it seems that if you and I could figure out a way to help you start to feel better about yourself when you are in science class, then things may start to get better?

Jerome: But how?

Reflection "in" Practice

Super! Jerome is starting to take real ownership for the situation, moving clearly into the contemplation stage. His "but how" suggests he is seeing the need and value of change and is now more receptive to taking some small steps toward that end. Maybe I can help him identify a step he could take in preparation of some real remedial action.

Ms. S: Well, if I understood what you said about your other classes, you feel good about yourself in those classes because you get good grades. So, maybe if we could figure out a way to improve your grades in science class, then you would feel good about yourself there as well. I wonder, do you have any ideas about what might help?

Jerome: I guess if I got better grades on my projects and, and . . . I guess I should do all my homework.

Ms. S: Hmm . . . the plot thickens (smiling). Are you saying you have some homework assignments that you are missing?

Jerome: Yeah, I think.

Ms. S: And, do you think if you completed the homework, then that would help your grades improve and maybe even give Ms. Pettigrew one less reason to correct you?

(Continued)

(Continued)

Jerome: Yeah (smiling), I guess.

Ms. S: Okay. Well, then that sounds like a good thing to try, but I'm wondering, do you have some ideas about what you could do maybe by Friday that may help?

Jerome: Well, I'm not sure what assignments I'm missing. I guess I could ask Ms. Pettigrew to let me know what I'm missing so that I could maybe start doing those over the weekend.

Reflection "in" Practice

That's a real commitment and it came from him. I think he's ready to make some preparations toward action.

Ms. S: Jerome, that's great. Boy. If you could find out what assignments you are missing, we would be able to make a plan that might help. Would you be able to do that, you know, go talk to Ms. Pettigrew and see if she will tell you all that needs to be done?

Jerome: I guess. But I'm not sure she'll tell me. She might just get mad and say something like if I did my homework when it was due, I wouldn't have a problem.

Reflection "in" Practice

Jerome is starting to invest in preparing for change, but he is also projecting some costs to this decision. It is not unusual for a student in the contemplation stage to experience some ambivalence about change. Maybe I can help reduce the perceived costs and help facilitate his movement toward preparation?

Ms. S: So, you are a little nervous that maybe if you go to Ms. Pettigrew she'll be angry, and rather than tell you what needs to be done, she'll just criticize you again?

Jerome: I guess she could.

Ms. S: Well, I guess she could. And, I could see why that certainly would make the task of asking her a lot more difficult. But Jerome, I'm wondering, has she done that to you or another student in the past?

Jerome: I don't know.

Ms. S: Well, have you had to ask her for help on any of your projects or labs?

Jerome: Yeah, all the time.

Ms. S: Well, how does she treat you when you have done that?

Jerome: She's always nice. She always tells us that she likes it when students let her know that they need help.

Ms. S: That's good. It seems to be evidence that would suggest she would be happy to be asked, and not criticize you. But, I'm wondering, can you think of anything else that might let you know that she would help you and not use this as an opportunity to criticize you?

Jerome: I guess. I mean, she says that when we are confused about something—even the grade we get—that she would love to meet with us and explain it. I know she did that with me when I was confused why I got a D on my machine project.

Ms. S: That's interesting. So you got a D and you actually went to ask her why? Wow. That's really super. What happened?

Jerome: She told me I needed more references, and a cover page and a personal opinion page. I did them and got a B.

Ms. S: Jerome, that's fantastic. I mean, here's a situation where your efforts to find out what was wrong really helped.

Jerome: Yeah. I was glad to get the B.

Ms. S: Now that you remember those things, what do you think about how she will respond if you go tell her that you really are trying to improve your grades, and that you would like to know what assignments you are missing?

Jerome: I guess she would do like she did with my machine project. She would meet with me during lunch and go through what I need to do.

Ms. S: Oh, okay. So, there really is very little chance that she will be negative or critical? It seems that she will most likely give you the information you need? And if that works out like it did for the machine project, it should help your grades?

Jerome: I think so.

Ms. S: So, what do you think?

Jerome: I guess it would be okay and I could ask her tomorrow.

Ms. S: That would great! Maybe we could get together on Friday and go over what you found out. How does that sound?

Jerome: Okay.

Ms. S: Well, let's get you back to class and I'll see you on Friday. Thanks for coming down (smiling).

Jerome: You're welcome . . . see you Friday (smiling).

(Continued)

(Continued)

Reflection "on" Practice (Following the Session)

I feel really good about that session. I wanted to establish a working relationship and I think I did. As I suspected, Jerome entered the session in the precontemplation stage, truly not seeing "his" problem. I think that contrasting his responses and behaviors in his other classes with the way he acts in science helped him to see his part of the problem. I am very happy that he started to think about small steps he can take and I think reducing the cost of asking for help helped tip the decisional balance. The fact that he is willing to invest in checking on missed assignments says to me that he is not only seeing the problem, but owns it and clearly wants some resolution. He has moved into the preparation stage and is at a place where I think, with some success, he will be open to a plan for action targeting increasing his academic achievement in science class.

Session 2: From Preparation to Action

We pick up the interaction after the initial exchanges in which Jerome shared that he spoke with Ms. Pettigrew and she told him that he really was only missing one homework assignment. Ms. Pettigrew explained to Jerome that homework incompletion was not what was holding his grade back, but that he needed to prepare better for the quizzes and tests.

Ms. S: Well, I am so proud of you. I know it was a little scary asking Ms. Pettigrew for help, but you did and, hey, only one homework missing. Whew!

Jerome: Yeah. She told me she was proud of me for trying to do better in class.

Ms. S: Well, I'm proud too. So, will you be able to get that homework completed?

Jerome: Yeah. I'm going to do it tonight, but . . .

Ms. S: But?

Jerome: Well, Ms. Pettigrew said that I have to do better on my tests and quizzes, and I'm not sure how. I don't know if I can do that.

Reflection "in" Practice

Jerome did very well and really has shown a commitment to change, but I'm concerned about his sense of self-efficacy, especially in terms of getting better grades on tests. If I could help him experience a little success, maybe I could get him to commit to some study techniques and even join the afterschool-tutoring program.

Ms. S: Well, you know what? Sometimes students just need to learn to relax a little when they are taking a test, or use some study tricks to help prepare for the test.

Jerome: Study tricks? What are study tricks?

Ms. S: Just a couple of things you can do to make studying a little easier and better. Maybe that's something you and I could work on.

Jerome: I guess, but I don't know if that will help.

Ms. S: Well, we won't know unless we try it. Maybe we could start slowly and try just a couple of things. How about the next time you have a quiz coming up, you let me know and I will show you some of those tricks?

Jerome: We have a quiz on Friday.

Ms. S: You do? Okay. Do you know what the quiz is going to be on?

Jerome: Yes. It's a vocabulary quiz from the chapter we are doing.

Ms. S: Well, how about if we try a few things. How about if you and I get together tomorrow during your study hall? All you need to do is bring your textbook, and if you have a chance tonight, maybe you could write each of the vocabulary words on one of these cards (handing Jerome a stack of 3 × 5 index cards), just one word per card. Can you do that?

Jerome: Sure.

Reflection "in" Practice

Jerome's willingness to "contract" with me to develop these study skills shows commitment. Given that he does so well in social studies and English, I have a feeling he just needs to relax and have a couple of successes. I think he will need a lot of verbal praise for his efforts and maybe I can get Ms. Pettigrew to give him a few pats on the back for trying and working hard, even if the quiz grade doesn't immediately improve.

Postscript

Ms. Shatz met with Jerome and helped him prepare for the quiz. The success he experienced served as a springboard for his committing to go to Ms. Pettigrew's afterschool study group, an experience that not only helped improve his grades but also allowed him to encounter Ms. Pettigrew outside of the classroom. This less than formal contact helped him develop a more positive attitude toward her.

CASE 2: KATHLEEN

Background

Kathleen, an eighteen-year-old senior, came to her counselor, Dr. Zimmerman, after trying on her own, for months, to stop smoking marijuana on weekends. Kathleen had decided to stop using marijuana as a recreational weekend drug three months ago, after receiving her acceptance to a premed college program. She has tried to say "no" to her friends, but is finding it difficult to be consistent.

Receiving the acceptance letter served as the "wake-up call" for Kathleen to get serious about her studies, and she is fully aware that over the course of the past year, smoking marijuana and hanging out with a select group of students who also smoke has been negatively affecting her attitude and motivation for school. Kathleen is a student who not only embraces her problem and sees the benefits of change, but also has given evidence of taking some initial steps to change, including now coming to Dr. Zimmerman's office for assistance. In this situation, the counselor wants to draw on those processes found to be effective in moving the client from preparation to action and maintenance (see Table 6.2).

Table 6.2   Stage-Process Integration

Case 2: Kathleen			
	Preparation	*Action*	*Maintenance*
Process of Change	Self-Liberation	Contingency Management Helping Relationships Stimulus Control Counterconditioning	

Session 1: From Contemplation to Action

Dr. Z: Hi Kathleen. Come on in.

Kathleen: Hi Dr. Z. Do you have a minute? I'd like to talk with you.

Dr. Z: Absolutely. Have a seat. What's up?

Kathleen: Well, I am not sure where to begin, but I think I need some help.

Reflection "in" Practice

Kathleen seems very nervous, but clearly she's coming with an agenda. At least, at a minimum level, she is aware of some area of concern and her presence here says that she is committed to change and has taken steps, like coming to me, as preparation for that change. I just need to go slow and allow her to relax, trust, and be heard.

Dr. Z: Kathleen, I can tell that you have something that you wish to share and I appreciate that you were willing to come down. There's no rush. You can start anywhere you wish.

Kathleen: I know. It's just a little strange. Anyway, you know I was accepted to Johns Hopkins for premed?

Dr. Z: I sure do, and I know how hard you worked to get there. Fantastic.

Kathleen: Yeah, but you may also know that my grades are kind of dropping off, a little.

Dr. Z: Well, nothing has been said to me by any of your teachers. Your grades are dropping?

Kathleen: Yeah, just a little. That's not the issue. I'm still okay grade wise, but I've noticed that I'm just not as motivated or interested in class, and I tried to figure out what's going on.

Dr. Z: So, you have been thinking about this for a while? Have you come to any conclusions?

Kathleen: Well, I think maybe I've been partying a little too much and it's starting to affect me.

Dr. Z: Partying?

Kathleen: Well, I . . . hmm . . . I've been hanging out with some people on the weekends and we get high and stuff.

Dr. Z: You get high and stuff? Could you tell me what you mean?

Kathleen: We kind of hang out at this one guy's apartment, and we drink beer and smoke marijuana.

Dr. Z: Oh, so when you say partying, you mean drinking beer and smoking marijuana, and you have doing this for the past few months on weekends. Have you been partying with any other drugs?

Kathleen: Oh, no, just the marijuana, not even the beer, that's what the other guys do.

Dr. Z: And just weekends?

Kathleen: Absolutely. And it's not every weekend, but it's most Fridays and Saturdays.

Dr. Z: Okay, and now you are concerned about how this partying might be affecting you?

Kathleen: Yeah. I don't know. When I got the letter from Hopkins it kind of, I don't know, woke me up? I mean, this is a big deal and I don't want to blow it, so I know I need to keep focused.

(Continued)

(Continued)

Reflection "in" Practice

Kathleen sounds very sincere and clearly wants assistance with restraining from such partying and staying focused. I wonder what she's tried, and what she hopes or expects from me. I think trying to get her to identify a clear, concrete goal, and maybe even doing some goal scaling, may be helpful ways to maintain her commitment and increase her hopefulness about a solution.

Dr. Z: I really appreciate you coming down, and I am really proud of you for taking control over your life. Since you said you have been working on this for some time, maybe you could tell me what you've been trying?

Kathleen: Yeah. I have been trying to stop but it seems like I do okay for a while, and then I blow it. It's really discouraging.

Reflection "in" Practice

Kathleen sounds a little discouraged. It may help if she understands that change does not always occur in clear, sequential, fixed steps, but tends to be a little cyclical, moving back and forth across the stages.

Dr. Z: I know it can be frustrating, even discouraging, when you really want to change and when you try really hard, but experience setbacks. But you know what? That is often how real change occurs—two steps forward, one back. So, the fact that you keep trying and the fact that you came here *is progress*!

Kathleen: Thanks.

Dr. Z: Well, just what have you tried to do to help you stop partying?

Kathleen: Well, I just kind of tried to stop, cold turkey, and I do real well, but then my friends keep bugging me just to come out for a little while, or come to this one special party, and then, poof, I'm there partying again.

Reflection "in" Practice

It does not sound like the issue is that Kathleen is craving marijuana; it is more like she has difficulty resisting the peer pressure, and then once in that social context, finds it hard to resist the partying. Maybe if we could clarify her goal, we could then do some goal scaling to move her toward the goal. I think the issue is social contact and she needs additional helping relationships to support her decision.

Dr. Z: Kathleen, I want you to try something. Let's pretend that tonight when you go home and go to sleep, a miracle happens while you are sleeping. It's the kind of miracle that when you wake, you immediately become aware that things are exactly like you want them to be. Okay, so it's a miracle. Now, when you wake up, what would you notice that would tell you that a miracle happened?

Kathleen: A miracle, hmm . . . well, I already had some of that with the Hopkins's acceptance (smiling). I guess, what I would notice, would be that I wasn't partying on weekends and that if my friends called me to party, I could say no and stick to it.

Dr. Z: Okay. So, if the miracle happened, you could say no to your friends and you wouldn't be partying, but if you weren't partying, what would you be doing instead?

Kathleen: I don't know. I guess I would just be at home?

Dr. Z: Well, that doesn't sound like a ton of fun, staying home by yourself.

Kathleen: I know, and that's why sometimes I just go out.

Reflection "in" Practice

Kathleen has a clear vision of what she would like to do, but saying no to her friends is costly in that her only option appears to be staying home alone if she doesn't go out. I want to help her expand her goal to envision a more desirable option to partying or staying home alone.

Dr. Z: Well, could you think of a time when you were able to say no to going out and partying because you had a better offer? You know, something that you really wanted to do?

Kathleen: You mean like other than staying home working on my college applications, or the night before the College Board exam, those kinds of things?

Dr. Z: Yeah, that works, but I'm wondering if you have had a time when you were doing something fun . . . something social, and because of that, you didn't want to go party?

Kathleen: Yeah. A couple of times, I've gone with my cousin and his friends to see a ball game, or when I was dating Jamie, we would go to movies and things.

Dr. Z: Perfect! So saying no is a lot easier when you know that there is something you have to do at home, like your college applications, or when you have something to do like go to a ball game with your cousin.

(Continued)

(Continued)

Reflection "in" Practice

So, there are some conditions that support her desire to say no. I'm wondering if we can break these down using a scaling technique.

Dr. Z: Kathleen, if I made a scale where 10 is when you no longer go out partying on the weekend but instead do things like go to dinner, movies, sporting events, and a 1 would be when you go out every night partying, where would you place yourself?

Kathleen: I guess I'm at a 4 or 5. I mean, I don't go out every night and not even every weekend. I also go out with my cousin when he calls.

Dr. Z: Great. So if that's a 4 or 5, what would a 6 or 7 look like?

Kathleen: I guess at a 6 or 7, I would be asking my friends to go out and do something with me, other than partying, or I would be asking other people to do things with me on weekends.

Reflection "in" Practice

Well, that sounds like a reasonable goal, and maybe achievable if we target just this weekend. I think Kathleen needs to experience success, and be reinforced for all her efforts. I also think if she feels she has a plan, she will feel more confident.

Dr. Z: Okay, that's great. Now, I am wondering about this coming weekend. Is there anything you would like to do, you know, is there anything for school you need to do, or any movie or concerts going on?

Kathleen: I don't know. I really haven't thought about it.

Dr. Z: I'm also wondering, can you think of anyone whom you would like to hang out with, assuming they are available this weekend?

Kathleen: Actually, as you're talking, I remember my cousin was talking about an American Hi-Fi concert on his campus and he wanted me to come up.

Dr. Z: Okay, so if you decide to go to the concert, would that be the support you need to say no to your friends about partying this weekend?

Kathleen: Yeah, definitely.

Reflection "in" Practice

Well, the social context is supportive of her saying no this weekend, but I really want her to start developing that sense of self-efficacy and belief that she can say no even when there is no ready-made excuse.

Dr. Z: So, do you feel pretty confident that this weekend will be party free?

Kathleen: Absolutely. My cousin and his friends are real straightedge.

Dr. Z: Straightedge?

Kathleen: Yeah. They have all agreed to be drug and alcohol free at all their parties and things.

Dr. Z: Wow, they sound like they would be a good group to hang with. And while that helps for this weekend, if I understood your goal and what you said, you really want to learn to be able to say no consistently. Is there anything you could do to not just avoid the party group, but maybe assert yourself so that you actually say no in a way that conveys you are not really interested in partying?

Kathleen: I'm not sure what you mean?

Dr. Z: Well, I guess I'm thinking I could see where someone could call you, and say there's a party, and you say something like, "No, I can't. I have something I have to do," or you could say something like, "No, I'm out of that partying stuff. I'm starting to hang out with some straightedgers," is that right? Anyway, something like that?

Kathleen: Wow. I'm not sure I could do that. That sounds like a 10 to me (smiling).

Dr. Z: That's fair. But you got the idea. Is there anything you could do that would be moving in that direction of really saying no?

Kathleen: Well, I could ask Abbey to go with me. She's a friend who does a lot of partying but she loves the bassist for American Hi-Fi, so she would probably want to go. I could ask her if she wants to come with me, and I could tell her it's a straightedge group and I'm trying to quit partying.

Reflection "in" Practice

Kathleen is really invested in change. It seems that identifying specific steps she could take to support her decision and also engage the helping relationships with her cousin, his friends, and maybe even Abbey, may really help.

Dr. Z: Boy, that would be fantastic. Not only would you be asserting yourself, but maybe you would be developing a different type of relationship with Abbey and maybe some of the other partying group.

Kathleen: Yeah, it would be cool if that happened. I mean, it is a lot easier to say no if I had friends that I could hang out with.

Dr. Z: You are right on, and I think that is something you and I could work on. But for now, how do you feel about the plan to maybe give Abbey a call and invite her to go to the concert with you, telling her that you are trying to do things that are not drug related?

(Continued)

(Continued)

Kathleen: I think I can do that . . . I really do (smiling).

Dr. Z: Would you like to get together on Monday and let me know how it went?

Kathleen: Sure.

Dr. Z: Plus, I'm wondering, would you like to start to put our heads together regarding that nonpartying social support that you could use?

Kathleen: That would be great. Thanks.

Reflection "on" Practice

Kathleen definitely came with a clear view of her problem and a real desire to change. She certainly was operating from the preparation stage where she had tried a couple of times to say no, with limited success. Clearly knowing that sometimes efforts to change regress before they progress, and having her set smaller goals seemed to help to empower her, as a self-liberating process. I think she's ready and able for action. Hopefully, this weekend will be successful and we can turn our attention to developing the helping relationships needed to support her desired change. Given her discouragement, I think it is important that I reinforce all small change and effort to affect that change. I think we need to also find ways to provide her prompts to say no, maybe using the acceptance letter from Hopkins, or pictures of doctors in action, as a way of keeping her goal in mind.

Session 2: Using Self and Environmental Evaluation

Kathleen: Hi Dr. Z.

Dr. Z: Hi Kathleen. Well, how was your weekend?

Kathleen: Fantastic (smiling). I went to concert and it was great. I had a great time and no partying!

Dr. Z: That's super, but how about the saying no part?

Kathleen: Oh, yeah, that was cool too. Abbey called me before I had a chance to call her, and I told her I wasn't going to party and was going to go up to my cousin's to see the concert. I invited her, and she said no . . . but it was cool. We had a really good discussion and I told her I was quitting smoking marijuana, and therefore wouldn't be partying. She thought that was great, and even said that she's getting tired of it, too. But I'm not really sure she meant it. But it was cool . . . I was able to really say out loud that I was done.

Dr. Z: That's fantastic. How do you feel having come clean with Abbey (smiling)?

Kathleen: I really felt good. I mean, I am not sure Abbey is going to stop partying, but I know we're still cool and at times when she's not partying, I know we can still hang out. And (smiling)...

Dr. Z: And, what?

Kathleen: Well, it appears that Jonathan, my cousin, has a new guy friend, Kris, who is really cool and we kind of it hit off, so it was definitely a good weekend (smiling).

Dr. Z: Well, it sounds like a great weekend, especially since you tested the water and found out that saying no most likely wouldn't result in you being rejected! And while I am happy that your cousin has nice friends (smiling), I really hope we could start to figure out how to get you connected with some people around here. I think the more social support you have for staying straight, the easier it will be.

The session continues, with a focus on: (1) identifying those people and situations that elicit partying behavior, and (2) establishing a number of alternative activities and people who Kathleen can engage as substitutes for partying. Dr. Zimmerman raises the issue of relapse, and together they decide that Kathleen will contact her cousin anytime she feels tempted. We pick up the session as it comes to an end.

Dr. Z: So, how do you feel about our plan?

Kathleen: I really think it can work. I'm amazed at all the things I loved to do, and the people with whom I used to do it. I really just got so into the partying that I forgot about all of that! I really feel like this is going to work.

Dr. Z: That's fantastic, and honestly, I think it can work as well. I would like to check in with you in a couple of weeks just to follow-up, and see how it's going. Okay?

Kathleen: Absolutely. But what happens if I screw up?

Dr. Z: Remember, I told you that sometimes we take a couple steps forward and maybe a step back. So, if you feel like you are being tempted to go party or you are finding it hard to say no, I really hope you call me, or like you said, call your cousin. Can you do that?

Kathleen: Yeah, I think so. I'll stop in just to give you thumbs up, if that's okay.

Dr. Z: I'd love it.

Postscript

Dr. Zimmerman saw Kathleen in the lunchroom on Monday and got a thumb's up. Later that week, Kathleen sent him an e-mail simply saying that she was looking into joining a community choir and was beginning to take tennis lessons. Both of these decisions and commitment of resources gave more evidence of her engagement in corrective action. The counselor was quick to reinforce and support those decisions, and invited her to continue to keep in touch via e-mail.

It appears that the counselor's timely use of processes such as goal setting, reinforcement of success, counterconditioning, and establishing helping relationships helped move Kathleen from preparation through to action and maintenance of her desired change.

FINAL THOUGHTS

In the final chapter, Chapter 7, you will once again be provided a case illustration. However, this time, in addition to observing a school counselor operating with an eclectic perspective and employing TTM as the integrating framework, you will be invited to participate in the reflective processes occurring throughout the sessions.

At various points in the case presentation, you will be asked to reflect on what is happening as well as what it is that you would do next in the process. The hope is that by stepping into the dialogue, you will be able to translate your understanding of the cognitive model into its application.

Practice in Procedural Thinking

7

The previous chapter presented examples of two counselors employing a transtheoretical model of change as their orientation to guide their reflections on the material being presented and their decisions in response to those data. The cases illustrated the counselors' procedural thinking as they responded to the material and information provided by the students. The current chapter invites you to move beyond simply observing the procedural thinking of a school counselor employing TTM as a operating framework, to actually engaging in that very process.

This final chapter provides the case of Randall. It is a case that illustrates a process of moving from the initial "hello" through to termination. As you read the case material, you will note places where the counselor, Ms. Schulman, reflects on the material gained in practice and uses that reflection to guide her decisions and actions. However, prior to viewing Ms. Schulman's reflections and decisions, you will be invited to use the principles and constructs of the transtheoretical model of change as the framework or lens through which to process the same student data being presented and anticipate the counselor's response. A brief overview of TTM's stage-process integration model (Table 7.1, as introduced in Chapter 5), as well as the empirically supported processes employed by a counselor with a TTM-operating framework (Table 7.2, as seen earlier in Chapter 2), are presented below to assist you in this process of reflecting on the case material presented, and anticipating the counselor's response. It is hoped that this practice in anticipating the counselor's reflections and response will help you move from understanding the concepts and constructs of TTM to employing this eclectic model to guide your own reflective practice.

Table 7.1 Stage-Process Integration

	Stages of Change				
	Precontemplation	*Contemplation*	*Preparation*	*Action*	*Maintenance*
Processes of Change	Consciousness Raising				
	Dramatic Relief				
	Environmental Reevaluation				
		Self-Reevaluation			
		Self-Liberation			
				Contingency Management	
				Helping Relationships	
				Counterconditioning	
				Stimulus Control	

Table 7.2 Processes Promoting Change

Focus (Experiential or Behavioral)	Process of Change	Description	Illustration
Experiential Processes of Change	Consciousness Raising	Increasing awareness about the causes, consequences, and cures for a particular problem behavior.	When confronted, student says everything is okay with his current grades, yet the grades clearly illustrate he is failing and in danger of not graduating.

Focus (Experiential or Behavioral)	Process of Change	Description	Illustration
	Self-Liberation	Acceptance of personal responsibility, commitment, and power.	Student who was thrown out of the basketball game admits that he "lost it" when his opponent began "trash talking," and as a result, he hurt his team.
	Social Liberation	Increasing social opportunities.	Counselor has instituted a "buddy system" assigning students who are very popular to serve as guides and buddies to facilitate social inclusion of new students. Or, salad bars are incorporated in the cafeteria as a way to promote health and dieting for students at risk.
	Dramatic Relief	Increasing emotional experiences, followed by reduced affect if appropriate action can be taken.	Student is able to express her feelings of guilt surrounding the accidental death of a friend after engaging in an expressive, art-therapy activity. Or, one finds relief from repressed anger by engaging in a role play.

(Continued)

Table 7.2 (Continued)

Focus (Experiential or Behavioral)	Process of Change	Description	Illustration
	Environmental Reevaluation	Affective and cognitive assessments of how the presence or absence of a personal habit affects one's social environment.	Student, as a result of empathy training, begins to understand the negative impact his aggressive attitude and behavior has on others, and subsequently, how the behavior leads to his own social isolation.
	Self-Reevaluation	Combination of both cognitive and affective assessments of one's self-image with and without a particular unhealthy habit.	Student comes to understand the fact that his own self-talk supporting his self-concept of being rejectable results in behavior (e.g., failing to make eye contact, head down, social withdrawal) that makes this self-concept self-fulfilling.
Behavioral Processes of Change	Stimulus Control	Removing cues for unhealthy habits and adding prompts for healthier alternatives.	Counselors post "motivational posters" to highlight celebrities promoting the value of "study," "cooperation," "goal setting," etc. Or, a decision is made to remove soda and candy vending machines from campus as a way of reducing sugar intake.

Focus (Experiential or Behavioral)	Process of Change	Description	Illustration
	Helping Relationships	Combination of caring, trust, openness, and acceptance as well as support for the healthy behavior change.	Student finds the counselor to be a safe, trusting, caring individual with whom he can share his most intimate concerns and be open to therapeutic feedback.
	Counterconditioning	Learning healthier behaviors that can substitute for problem behaviors.	Student with test anxiety is taught relaxation techniques. Or, the student susceptible to peer pressure is taught assertive strategies. Or, the obese student is helped with identifying and employing replacement foods for those that are detrimental.
	Reinforcement Management	Providing consequences for taking steps in a particular direction.	Counselor helps the student establish a plan for increasing study time, using "video game playing time" as contingent on engaging in thirty minutes of studying.
	Self-Liberation	Believing that one can change along with the commitment and recommitment to act on that belief.	Student develops a "contract" with his parents stating that when he gets honors, they will allow him his license to drive a car. The contract serves as a public commitment to both the goal and the action needed to achieve the goal.

Prior to presenting the case, there is one final point to note. This case of Randall, the sixth-grade bully, is employed in the companion texts within this series. The reason for this replication is that it will provide readers the opportunity to compare and contrast the reflections and practice decisions of this one school counselor as she employs varying operational frameworks to guide her practice decisions.

CASE 1: RANDALL: THE SIXTH-GRADE BULLY

History and Context

Tammy Schulman is the middle school counselor at E. L. Richardson Middle School. Ms. Schulman receives a referral from the assistant principal that reads:

> Tammy, I've been hearing numerous complaints from teachers and students about Randall Jenkins. While we are only three weeks into the school year, Randall has already accrued ten demerits for fighting. It is clear that unless we do something, Randall won't be here by midterm. Please see him as soon possible.

Reflection "on" Practice

> Assuming you are a school counselor with an eclectic perspective and employing a transtheoretical model of change, what immediate "hypothesis" might you have about your first meeting with Randall, and what goal would you set for that encounter?

As Ms. Schulman sits at her desk, she attempts to envision Randall's reaction to "being sent" to the counselor. She anticipates that he might be somewhat defensive and enter counseling in the precontemplation stage. If this is the case, she wants to target those skills needed to establish a meaningful working alliance, one supporting rather than challenging him, and one that encourages him to share his own story. Allowing him to share his side of the story will demonstrate at least some "ownership" over the situation, and may open him to contemplating the need to address these issues.

Session 1: From Precontemplation to Contemplation

Ms. S: Randall, come in, and thanks for coming, I'm Ms. Schulman, the sixth-grade counselor.

Randall: (Looks down, and sits without talking.)

Ms. S: Randall, do you know why I asked you to come down and see me?

Randall: (Still looking down, and shows little response.)

Ms. S: Randall, you look a little uncomfortable, are you mad at me for some reason?

Randall: (Looks up, somewhat surprised by the question.)

Ms. S: Thanks for looking up. I wasn't sure if I was doing something wrong, because you look really unhappy. Are you unhappy right now?

Randall: (Nods yes, still not talking.)

Reflection "in" Practice

While it is very early in the interaction, what do you feel Ms. Schulman may be "thinking" and deciding to do? (Hint: Think about the processes that are employed to facilitate movement from precontemplation to contemplation.)

Ms. Schulman can see that Randall is either unaware or resisting any real ownership over this problem. It is clear that he is feeling uncomfortable at this moment. Trying to engage him in an action planning or remedial steps will be less than useful. Ms. Schulman knows she needs to keep creating a safe, supportive environment where he will be open to her feedback and gentle confrontation. Without his increased awareness (consciousness raising) of both the actual facts of the situation and his own feelings (dramatic relief) tied to what's been happening, progress will be slow. She wonders if she can probe his feelings in order to provide some relief and gain some value for their interaction.

Ms. S: Randall, I am really sorry that you are unhappy. I wish I could help. I can see that this is upsetting (softly). That's okay. Could you tell me how you are feeling, right now?

Randall: Uh-huh (holding back tears).

Ms. S: Take your time. It's okay. I know this can be hard.

Randall: It's just that everybody is on my case (starting to cry). Everybody's saying I have a problem (agitated). I don't have a problem. They're all picking on me.

Reflection "in" Practice

Randall is clearly upset and sounds angry. He has moved from the quiet defensive posture to at least providing some minimal verbal response. At this point, sensing his immediate problem of being "unhappy" and apparently defensive, what might your next move be if the goal is to move him to a contemplation stage of change?

(Continued)

(Continued)

Randall is clearly upset and expressing his strong sense of frustration and isolation. Ms. Schulman hopes that this experience of dramatic relief will allow him to begin to make a commitment to doing things differently. She thinks she needs to allow him to continue his story, and maybe take every opportunity to highlight his unhappiness and the subtle ways he may be contributing to this unhappiness, or at least help him begin to see that he has the ability, the power, to do something to make the situation the way he desires.

Ms. S: So, everyone is saying that you have a problem? Can you tell me more about that?

Randall: None of the kids like me, and they always say I'm starting problems, and Dr. Kim and my teachers tell me I'm a bully and need help (crying).

Ms. S: Randall, it must be really hard to hear Dr. Kim and your teachers say that you are bullying the other kids. I bet it makes you really sad that the other kids won't let you join in. I can see how upsetting it is for you.

Randall: Uh-huh (crying).

Ms. S: I'm wondering if maybe you and I can figure out what's going on?

Randall: But I'm not doing anything!

Reflection "in" Practice

Randall is still unaware, or unwilling, to take some ownership over this situation (precontemplation), but he is clearly upset and feeling very vulnerable. At this early stage of counseling, what would your goals be, assuming you are employing a TTM-counseling model?

Ms. Schulman observes that Randall is still unaware or unwilling to take some ownership over this situation (precontemplation), but he is clearly upset and feeling very vulnerable. She thought he was showing signs of moving toward contemplation, but also acknowledges that it's one or two steps forward, and one back. She reminds herself to go slowly, and be supportive, but also see if she can introduce some of the "facts" in order to help him to take some responsibility (contemplation).

Ms. S: Randall, I know it's upsetting to you, but I'm a little confused. I was talking to Dr. Kim, and he was telling me that you have had a problem with some of the other kids in school. Is that correct? That you are having a little problem with some of the students?

Randall: I guess . . . but it's not my fault (looking down).

Ms. S: It would really help if you could tell me a little about what has been going on? Like I know you said it's not your fault, but I'm not sure what the "it" is?

Randall: Fighting.

Ms. S: Oh, okay. Fighting. You mean you have gotten in some fights with the other students?

Randall: Yeah (looking down).

Reflection "in" Practice

Now that Randall has taken some ownership for "a" problem, what data would you like to gather, and/or which direction would you like to take? At this early stage of counseling, what would your goals be assuming you are employing a transtheoretical model of change? Which of the empirically supported processes might you employ?

Randall has made some initial movement, and Ms. Schulman is pleased that he is at least taking some ownership over fighting, but his tone and his looking down tells her that he may not be ready to fully embrace the problem as his responsibility. She wonders if she can get him to describe a recent situation so that maybe she could pose questions that may get him to see his role in all of this.

Ms. S: Fighting. Hmm. You know what? It would really help me if you could tell me about one of the specific situations or events that got you into some trouble?

Randall: You mean like when I was sent down to see Dr. Kim?

Ms. S: Sure, if you wouldn't mind telling me what happened?

Randall: I was sent to Dr. Kim on Monday because Boston and I were pushing each other in lunch line. And last week, I went to Dr. Kim because Chuck Hammel and I got into an argument in the bathroom and then started pushing each other, until Mr. Allison stopped it.

Ms. S: Oh, so you had two recent situations, one with Boston, I assume you mean Ralph Boston, and one with Chuck Hammel. Okay. Would you mind telling me a little more about one of these situations, maybe the one with Ralph Boston?

Reflection "in" Practice

While we are not sure if Randall will be able to accurately report on these incidents, what do you think Ms. Schulman may be looking for? Or, how might she use these data? What, if any, benefit will having Randall relate these incidents bring, if the goal is to facilitate his movement through the stages of change?

(Continued)

(Continued)

Ms. Schulman hopes that the details of the incident with Ralph will allow her to reflect and highlight Randall's involvement in the process as a way to raise his consciousness of his problem and ground him in the contemplation stage of change. She also believes that her attending and nonjudgmental style, and conveyance of a sense of hope, may also allow him to experience some dramatic relief.

Randall: Well, Boston just cut in front of me in lunch line and he said real loud so everybody could hear it, "What are you lookin' at, loser?" Then the other kids in line started making noises like "oooh" and saying things like "get him," that kind of stuff.

Ms. S: So Ralph just cut in front of you, and called you a name, and then the other kids started to encourage you to do something?

Randall: Yeah, and then Boston, I mean Ralph, just kept looking at me and then said something like, "You want to do something about it, homo?" And then I got really angry and pushed him.

Ms. S: So, he called you more names and then you got really angry and pushed him. Would it be okay if I wrote that down?

Randall: I guess.

Ms. S: It will help me. Let me see if I understand it (starting to write down as she speaks). So you are in lunch line, and then Ralph jumps into line ahead of you and then he makes this comment of, "What are you lookin' at, loser?" and the other kids started to make noises . . . is that pretty much the picture?

Randall: Yeah. He really made me mad. I wanted to show him.

Ms. S: So, okay. Let me write that down over here. You said you were really mad and you wanted to show him, so you pushed him. Is that right?

Randall: Yeah, and I would have punched him if Mr. Jacobs didn't pull us out of line. He told us to go see Dr. Kim.

Ms. S: Hmm, okay. I think I got that. So, Boston started the name-calling and the butting in line, and the other kids were trying to get you all worked up and I guess it worked.

Randall: Worked?

Ms. S: Well, if they wanted to get you all worked up and get you in trouble, they did. It seems you got really mad and then because you started pushing Ralph, you are the one who got in trouble. Is that right?

Randall: Yeah (getting upset). But why are they always picking on me? He's the one that should have gotten in trouble, not me.

Reflection "in" Practice

There was a little movement, for at least Randall agreed he pushed first and is giving a little evidence that the "rejection" hurts. Now, what would you do? Is Randall still in the precontemplation stage or has he moved toward contemplation?

Ms. Schulman notes that Randall came close by admitting to pushing, and his tone clearly shows that he's sad about the kids making fun of him. She decides there may be a way to reframe this situation so that he sees that he is giving away his power to silly name-calling, and that he's the one who is actually paying the price. She hopes she can get him to think about taking the steps needed to take that power back (contemplation). She thinks that if she can find a little more evidence of his giving away the power, she can confront him with a gentle summarization.

Ms. S:	I think I understand what happened with Ralph. I have some ideas, but let me know a little more about the situation with Chuck, and then I'll tell you what I'm thinking. Okay?
Randall:	Okay. Well, it was after gym, and I went to the bathroom and a couple of other guys from gym were in there and Chuck said, real loud as I walked in, "Hey loser, who invited you?" and then everybody started to laugh.
Ms. S:	So, the other guys started to laugh? What happened next?
Randall:	I was going to the stall, and Chuck was going to the sink, and he gave me a shove.
Ms. S:	So he pushed you first?
Randall:	Well, he kind of bumped into me as we passed, but then he called me a name and the other guys started to yell "get him" and I just pushed him into the sink.
Ms. S:	Oh, so he called you a name, and then other guys started encouraging you to do something and you pushed him?
Randall:	Yeah, and that's when Mr. Allison came in and told me to go to Dr. Kim's office.
Ms. S:	That's wild. Can you see anything common in these two situations?
Randall:	Yeah. I pushed them.
Ms. S:	Well that's one thing. Anything else?
Randall:	They started it by calling me a loser or something.

(Continued)

(Continued)

Ms. S: Randall, good job. Yep, it seems that they called you names. How about anything else that was happening in both situations?

Randall: You mean like the other kids were saying things like "get him" and making noises?

Ms. S: Wow. Fantastic. I mean, you are right on. In both situations, it seems that the guys were calling you a name, like loser or something, and then the other students who were watching started to make noises and tell you to push them and things like that. And then you get very angry and start pushing . . . hmm. Seems like they know how to push your buttons?

Randall: I guess (looking down). I kind of have a short fuse. But they really pissed me off. Sorry.

Reflection "in" Practice

We now have two illustrations of Randall getting angry, and he is admitting to having a short fuse. Are we entering contemplation? Is he ready for some small steps in preparation? Now, how would you proceed? What would you like to accomplish before the end of this session?

Randall has taken some ownership over these incidents, but Ms. Schulman is not sure if he sees the need or value to changing this "short fuse." She wonders if she can get him to do a little homework as a way to increase his value on the need to change and move to the contemplation stage.

Ms. S: Randall, that's okay. But I'm a bit confused. You seem like a pretty smart guy, and so I'm confused as to why you would give these students so much power over you?

Randall: I don't give them anything.

Ms. S: Well, if I understood what you said, it appears that you feel that the other students are the ones getting you in trouble?

Randall: I told you. They piss me off (sounding annoyed).

Ms. S: No. I understood that is what you said, but that's exactly what I meant. If they really have the power to make you angry and get you in trouble, I guess I'm wondering why a guy like you hasn't decided to take that power back.

Randall: I don't get what you are saying.

Reflection "in" Practice

Cleary, Ms. Schulman has stimulated some "confusion," or some cognitive dissonance. Where would you go at this point in the interaction? What do you anticipate she will do with this confusion?

Ms. Schulman feels she has stimulated curiosity, and this may serve as a motivation to engage Randall in the counseling. Rather than simply addressing his behavior, she feels it is important to get him to begin thinking about his behavior and see if he can discover some personal value in coming to counseling.

Ms. S: I guess it can be a bit confusing. But, you know how you said you have a short fuse?

Randall: Yeah.

Ms. S: Well, it seems that the other guys have figured out how to set off your fuse.

Randall: Uh-huh.

Ms. S: So, that's what I mean by taking your power back. You know, figuring out how to make sure your fuse can't be set off.

Randall: How do you do that?

Ms. S: That's a great question, and I have some ideas about that. But for now, we should get you back to class. How about if I get you out of study hall tomorrow, and I'll show you what I mean and see if it is something you would like to do?

Randall: I don't get it, but okay.

Ms. S: Okay, hang in there (smiling). We can talk about it tomorrow. You could help, though, if you could begin to think about a couple of other times when your "short fuse" really didn't work. You know, a time or situation when the short fuse really cost you. Could you do that?

Randall: That's easy. I got thrown out of the championship game 'cause I lost my cool.

Ms. S: Ouch. That's a good example that we can talk about tomorrow—good job. Maybe there are others?

Randall: I'll think about it.

Ms. S: See you tomorrow!

Randall: Okay, see ya.

(Continued)

(Continued)

Reflection "on" Practice

It is clear that Randall is both confused and a bit curious. As you reflect on the session and in anticipation of the upcoming session, what would be your goals for this next session? How would you build on his confusion over the issue of taking the power back? What does his willingness to give an example of his short fuse costing him suggest about his progression through the change process? How do you build on that?

As Ms. Schulman reflects, she concludes that while Randall was not as enthusiastic as she would like, he was at least open to coming back, and coming back with his own issue rather than one that was imposed on him. She concludes that he is a bright guy, and his willingness to share a personal example of when his short fuse cost him (i.e., being thrown out of the game) may suggest that he is seeing this as "his" problem and may be positioning himself to take some action. The focus for the next session will be to see if he came up with other "costs" of his short fuse, and then contrast that with a preferred scenario when he was in control of his temper. Maybe using his examples, along with the situations at school, to highlight how his fuse is costing him will tip the decisional balance and he might be more interested in taking some small steps in preparation for change.

Session 2: From Preparation to Action

Ms. S: Good morning, Randall. How are you?

Randall: Okay. We have baseball tryouts today so I'm kind of excited.

Ms. S: Oh, that's right. You told me you were quite a pitcher?

Randall: Yeah. I'm pretty good.

Ms. S: Well, you'll have to let me know how it goes. I am wondering, how did you feel after we got together yesterday?

Randall: Okay.

Ms. S: Okay?

Randall: Yeah. I guess it was good.

Ms. S: Well, when we stopped, I was asking you about times when losing your cool may have cost you, and you started to tell me about getting kicked out of a game? Would you tell me about that?

Randall: Yeah (smiling). Last year, when I was playing basketball for my community recreation team, we were in the championship game and this kid was guarding me and trash talking and . . .

Ms. S: I'm sorry, "trash talking"?

Randall: Yeah. He was telling me I was slow, and dribbled like a girl, and stuff like that.

Ms. S: Okay. So, he was kind of making fun of you.

Randall: Yeah, and he kept up. I told him to shut up, and he just got worse, like if I missed a shot, he would say things like, "Nice shot, retard" or, "I bet your sister plays better, loser." Stuff like that.

Ms. S: Got it. But how did you get kicked out?

Randall: Well, he kept it up and kept calling me a loser, and a "spaz" and stuff like that, and so he was mouthing off and I pushed him down, and we got into a fight and we were both ejected.

Ms. S: So, he kept calling you names like "loser," and that made you get really angry, and then you lost control and got kicked out of the game. I bet your coach wasn't real happy about that?

Randall: No. I'm one of the best players on the team and this other kid was okay, but not real good, so getting me kicked out really hurt our team.

Ms. S: Oh, so I see why you said that's a time when your temper cost you . . . and your team?

Randall: Well, we won the championship anyway, but I could have been the most valuable player of the game . . . and lost that because I didn't play the whole last quarter.

Ms. S: Well, glad you won the championship, but that's really a shame about the MVP award. So I guess that temper thing can be pretty darn costly to you?

Randall: Yeah.

Reflection "in" Practice

Randall has certainly presented a very clear example of the cost of his temper. Do you feel he is owning the problem sufficiently to move him through contemplation to preparation? Where would you go next?

(Continued)

(Continued)

As Ms. Schulman reflects on these data, she concludes that while Randall gave a great example of the cost of his anger, the example was somewhat remote, being last year, and she wonders if there is something more recent that she can point to in order to tip his decisional balance.

Ms. S: Randall, that is really a great example, but I'm wondering if you could think of a more recent time when your anger really cost you?

Randall: You mean like with Ralph and Chuck?

Ms. S: That's really good. Yesterday, when we were talking about those situations, I didn't think you saw that as something that cost you. Could you tell me what you are thinking about those things, now?

Randall: Well, my mom gave me an earful last night and told me if I kept getting into trouble that she won't let me go out for the school team this year. So, if I get into any more problems with fighting and stuff, I'm off the team and that would really stink.

Ms. S: Got it! So, even if someone teases you and calls you a loser, like that guy during the championship game, or like Ralph and Chuck did, you need to have control or it really will cost you.

Randall: Yeah. I really want to play, but I'm worried that I will just flip out and lose it if these guys start up again.

Reflection "in" Practice

Randall seems to be indicating that he is concerned about his ability to control his temper. That seems to suggest that he sees the need to change (contemplation), but is now unsure of his own ability to do so. What steps would you take to move him into the preparation stage? How might processes such as goal setting, scaling, or targeting self-efficacy be useful?

Randall clearly wants to change, but with his history, Ms. Schulman wonders if controlling his temper seems to him to be almost impossible. She would like to support his sense of self-efficacy, and decides that one way may be to go back to the championship game and see if maybe he could find an "exception" to this explosive tendency, since finding an exception might help him believe he can do it. If he sees that he has and can do it, Ms. Schulman reflects, then all he will need is a plan to be better at doing it.

Ms. S: Randall, it sounds like you not only really want to play, but that you really want to learn how to control your temper?

Randall: Yeah, but I don't know if I can.

Ms. S: I understand your concern, and I recognize it might seem like a hard habit to break. But I was thinking about your championship game, and I was really interested in something. You said you lost your cool in the fourth quarter, is that right?

Randall: Yeah, that's when I got thrown out!

Ms. S: But, didn't you say that this guy was calling you names, and trying to get you all fired up, for most of the game?

Randall: Yeah. I was scoring pretty well and he was having trouble guarding, so by the second quarter, he started trash talking.

Ms. S: That's fantastic.

Randall: What is?

Ms. S: Well, if he was trash talking to you for all of the second quarter and all of the third quarter and most of the fourth quarter, then you must have been doing something really good to keep yourself under control. I mean, you didn't get angry and push him until late in the fourth quarter, right?

Randall: Yeah. It was only like three or four minutes to go.

Ms. S: Wow. If we could figure out how you did that, you know, how you kept your cool, then we could figure out a way that you could do that more often!

Randall: Oh, okay. I didn't think about it like that!

Ms. S: Well, we have to get you back to class, but I think we are on to something. Would you like to work on this?

Randall: Yeah. I really want to play baseball this year and I don't want to blow that.

Ms. S: Randall, I can hear how important it is to you, and I really feel good knowing that there are times when you can ignore the teasing and just hold your temper. So, let's get together Monday and put our heads together. Okay?

Randall: Yeah.

Ms. S: How about over the weekend, you try to think of some other exceptions. I mean, other times when someone was trying to set your fuse, like that guy was trying to do during the basketball game, but you ignored it or did something that helped you to stay calm and focused. Could you do that?

Randall: Yeah. You mean like there was a time when I was playing basketball in my driveway and my older brother started shooting with me, and as we played, he started cutting up on me, but I just laughed it off.

(Continued)

(Continued)

Ms. S: That is fantastic! That's exactly what we are looking for, so when we get together, we are going to try to figure out what you did with your brother or what you did during the first three quarters of that championship game that allowed you to be cool. Okay?

Randall: Yeah (smiling).

Reflection "on" Practice

This was quite an exchange. Given the apparent enthusiasm Randall is exhibiting, what do you feel your goals and plans might be for the next session? Does the fact that he has begun to think of "exceptions" suggest that he is in the preparation stage and ready for action?

Ms. Schulman decides that Randall is ready for action. She sees that he is an engaging, bright student and she thinks he's starting to see that he has the power to control his anger, and also has concrete, successful experiences that demonstrate that he can do it. She wants to continue reviewing his exceptions and help him identify what he does, at those times, that helps him to maintain his cool. She thinks that is where they can find the answer.

Session 3: Ready for Action

Ms. S: So? How did you do with our "homework"?

Randall: I couldn't think of any other times (smiling).

Ms. S: Well, that's okay, at least you thought about it.

Randall: Yeah, but something cool happened.

Ms. S: Really?

Randall: Yeah, we had a baseball game on Saturday, and I was pitching. I was pitching and the guys on the other team were trying to get me angry so that I would lose it, and then I wouldn't be able to pitch.

Ms. S: So they were trying to set your fuse?

Randall: Yeah, they were yelling things, like, "Nice throw, spaghetti arm" or, " You call that a fast ball?" and oh yeah, the one I like and I am going to use on other pitchers, was, "Didn't you play on the girls' softball team?" Sometimes they say pretty bad things, but our coach doesn't let us do that.

Ms. S: Spaghetti arm? Pretty creative (smiling). So, they were trying to set your fuse by calling you names. Did it work?

Randall: No. I know they are trying to get me off my game so I just say to myself, "focus,"' and then I pitched harder and if I struck one of them out I would just smile at their bench (smiling).

Ms. S: Cool. So, when you were on the field, you took the power back (smiling), and you put your fuse away? I mean, here are these guys calling you names, even some that are really bad, but you just keep thinking or saying to yourself, "focus." And just thinking that helps keep you from getting all worked up? Is that how you do it?

Randall: Yeah.

Ms. S: That's cool. They had no power. Their words were just words, with no power.

Randall: Yeah. I knew what they were trying to do and so it didn't bother me.

Ms. S: So, you hear them say these things and you just say to yourself, "I know what they are trying to do. I'm not going to let them get me upset. I'm just going to focus," or something like that?

Randall: Yeah, I guess.

Ms. S: That's fantastic. It seems that when you know the other guys are trying to get you to lose your temper and you know, like in the case of the game, if you lose your temper you lose and they win, that at those times you can keep it together.

Randall: Yeah, 'cause I didn't want to get kicked out of the game.

Ms. S: Exactly. But I'm wondering about the situation in the lunch line. Wasn't Boston just trying to get you to lose it, and maybe get in trouble?

Randall: I guess, but it wasn't like when I was playing in the game. It just kind of happened.

Ms. S: I know it kind of caught you off guard, but I bet if Ralph was on the other team, and he was saying those things while you were pitching (smiling), you would walk off the mound and punch him?

Randall: No way (smiling)!

Ms. S: Yep. So maybe what we can work on is helping you remember that when the guys do this, they really are just trying to get you thrown out of the game!

Randall: But how can I do that?

(Continued)

(Continued)

Reflection "in" Practice

Randall is certainly engaged. He has given us some good material to work with. His question at the end certainly suggests he is ready for action. What strategies might you use during this action stage?

Ms. Schulman is really impressed by Randall's ability to identify the baseball incident as exactly the type they were looking for, and his willingness to think about the homework and actually do it shows he is ready for action. She thinks he needs help identifying the triggers, the cues that stimulate his response, and then she can begin to teach him an alternative response to those cues.

Ms. S: Randall, I guess if we could put baseball hats on all the guys who tease you, it may be easy for you to remember to stay cool (smiling)?

Randall: Yeah (smiling).

Ms. S: Well, you have to get back to class, but I have a little homework.

Randall: Ugh.

Ms. S: No, not that type of homework. I want you think about the types of names that guys could call you that seem to trigger your angry response. You know, like "loser," and "wimp," I think that was two?

Randall: Yeah. There are others, but some are bad.

Ms. S: Well, that's okay. You can tell me in here and we will figure out how to help you respond in different ways, even when they call you those things. That way (smiling), we can "keep you in the game!"

Randall: Okay. I can do that.

Ms. S: Great. Now, I can't see you tomorrow, but I will call you down on Thursday during study hall, okay?

Randall: Okay.

Reflections "on" Practice

TTM suggests that processes like stimulus control, reinforcement, counter-conditioning, and establishing helping relationships are effective for working with students in the action stage, through maintenance. Given how this relationship has unfolded, how might you use some of the above listed processes to assist Randall?

Ms. Schulman wants to see if she can get Randall to pair his image of a baseball hat, or being in a game, with these words that seem to trigger his response, perhaps by role playing some situations. She also wants to see if he has experienced the effect of ignoring or laughing off the comments. She hopes that he has seen how just ignoring these comments actually stops the guys from doing it. If it isn't working, why would they bother?

Session 4: Supporting Change and "Staying in the Game"

Ms. Schulman employed role-playing activities to desensitize Randall to the name-calling. In this fourth session, Randall is able to describe how the kids in the dugout actually stopped when he ignored them and he began to see the value of just laughing off the name-calling. We pick the session up as it is drawing to a conclusion.

Ms. S: Boy, it is really cool that, when you keep reminding yourself that they are just trying to get you thrown out of the game, you can stay cool?

Randall: Yeah? But how can I remember to do that at lunch or in class?

Ms. S: That's a great question. You know, it's really just a habit, and I'm wondering if we could come up with some reminders to help you "stay in the game"?

Randall: Maybe I could write that on my notebook?

Ms. S: You mean, "stay in the game"?

Randall: Yeah, I guess.

Ms. S: Randall, that is a super idea! Boy, if you look down and see a reminder to "stay in the game," I bet it would help you to stay calm and ignore the name-calling. That is really fantastic.

Randall: I'll try.

Session 4 concludes with some general discussion about the tryouts for the school baseball team, and the fact that Randall actually made the first string and will be starting.

Session 5: Targeting Maintenance

Ms. S: So, how did the "stay in the game" reminder work?

Randall: Well, I didn't really use it. I mean, I wrote it on my binder and copybook, and I did see it and I kind of kept thinking about it, but there was only one time when somebody said something and that was no big deal.

Ms. S: Only one time and it was not a big deal? Could you tell me about it?

(Continued)

(Continued)

Randall: Chuck just started getting on me after baseball practice yesterday. He was saying things like, "Hey newbie, be sure to clean my cleats," and then said real loud so that the rest of team heard him, "Hey, should newbie get us all some drinks?" and everybody laughed.

Ms. S: Wow. So, he was saying this in front of the team and you didn't get mad? How did you do that?

Randall: I don't know. It was just the stuff that goes when you are new on the team and everybody knew I was going to be starter, so it was cool.

Ms. S: Okay, got it. You didn't get angry, because you were feeling good about yourself and you knew that you were new to the team. I guess that's what they meant by newbie. But even being new, you felt pretty good because you were starting, so Chuck's comments didn't really mean anything?

Randall: Yeah. I am going to be in the pitching rotation and play right field when I'm not pitching. I'm psyched.

Reflection "in" Practice

Randall is feeling pretty good and apparently had quite a good week. What would be your goals for the counseling at this stage of the relationship?

Randall certainly has had a good week, and even though he didn't need to use the stimulus cue to stay in the game, he wrote it down and thought about it. Ms. Schulman wants to reinforce the potential value for such cues. Also, the fact that he made the baseball team as a starter should give him some status and provide him a support group. She wants to support him and let him know that she is there if he wants to talk.

Ms. S: That's really great stuff. You know, it seems like you had a really good week. Do you know what made it so good?

Randall: Yeah. I made the team.

Ms. S: That's true, but I have a feeling something else made it good?

Randall: You mean that I didn't lose my temper?

Ms. S: That . . . and?

Randall: I don't know. That Chuck and I were hanging out and goofing off.

Ms. S: Yep . . . and?

Randall: Ah, there's more?

Ms. S: Yep, and that you used the reminder, you know, writing it down on your notebook and thinking about it. Oh, also that you were feeling pretty good about yourself . . . all of these things made for a good week.

Randall: Yeah, it did. It was the best week I've had at school so far.

Ms. S: Well, I think that's super, but I'm wondering, what do you think you could do now to make next week and the following week good? You know, what steps can you take to make sure that fuse can't be lit and that you keep your temper under control?

Randall: I'm going to keep the sign I made about staying in the game on my binder and I even have one on my desk at home.

Ms. S: That's a great idea. That really is a great idea. I'm wondering about the guys on the baseball team. I mean, it seems you are hanging out more with them. Will that help with your temper?

Randall: Yeah. Actually, they all know that if I get in trouble, my mom won't let me play, and they all really want me on the team, so I think they will help me stay cool if I start to lose my temper.

Ms. S: That sounds like a great plan! I don't know what you think, but I think we did a fantastic job (smiling and giving Randall a high five).

Randall: Yep (smiling).

The session continues with the counselor complementing Randall on his active participation in the counseling and reminds him that she is there anytime he wanted to pop in and talk or tell her something. She also promises to come out and see him pitch.

Reflection "on" Practice

Things have certainly improved. Randall has transitioned from a precontemplation stage of change through to action, and even maintenance. What goals, if any, would you have at this point in the counseling process?

Ms. Schulman really feels good about the work they did, and she thinks Randall is in a good position to "keep his cool," but she also knows that relapses do occur. She hopes Randall will feel comfortable dropping in if he has a relapse, but thinks she will go check him out at a game the next week, or, in the next couple of weeks, go see him and the guys a lunch. She wants to keep reinforcing that cue to "stay in the game."

Follow-Up

Ms. Schulman went to see Randall pitch, and he was thrilled to have her there. As she was watching the game, Chuck, who was playing third base, made an error and the other team scored. Chuck began to act out, kicking the dirt, and smacking his glove; he looked like he was ready for a meltdown, and to Ms. Schulman's surprise, the entire bench started to give him support, saying, "No problem," "Get it next time," *and,* "Chuck, stay in the game!" Apparently, Randall's cue had become the team's motto—an event that certainly will reinforce that idea in Randall's mind.

Epilogue

A Beginning . . . Not an End

While we have come to the end of this book, it is hopefully only the beginning of your own ongoing development as a reflective school counselor. The material presented in this book has provided you with an introduction to the world of a eclectic school counselor, and the procedural thinking that guides his or her practice. However, it is truly just the beginning.

As school counselors, we know the value of maintaining competence in the skills we use and we know the ethical mandate to continue to develop those skills (See Resource, Standard E.1.c). While being open to new procedures demonstrated to be effective for the diverse population with whom we work, we must also recognize the limitations of our professional competence to use these procedures (see Resource, Standard E.1.a). The material provided in this book is but a first step to developing that competency.

Becoming an expert in counseling, as is true of any profession, requires continued training, personal reflection, and supervision. It is hoped that with this introduction to the theory and practice of an eclectic counselor, you will be stimulated to continue in that training, personal reflection, and supervision and as a result grow in thinking and acting like an expert.

Resource

*Ethical Standards
for School Counselors*

The American School Counselor Association's (ASCA) Ethical Standards for School Counselors were adopted by the ASCA Delegate Assembly, March 19, 1984, revised March 27, 1992, June 25, 1998 and June 26, 2004. For a PDF version of the Ethical Standards visit www.schoolcounselor.org/content.asp?contentid=173.

PREAMBLE

The American School Counselor Association (ASCA) is a professional organization whose members are certified/licensed in school counseling with unique qualifications and skills to address the academic, personal/social, and career development needs of all students. Professional school counselors are advocates, leaders, collaborators, and consultants who create opportunities for equity in access and success in educational opportunities by connecting their programs to the mission of schools and subscribing to the following tenets of professional responsibility:

- Each person has the right to be respected, be treated with dignity, and have access to a comprehensive school counseling program that advocates for and affirms all students from diverse populations regardless of ethnic/racial status, age, economic status, special needs, English as a second language or other language group, immigration status, sexual orientation, gender, gender identity/expression, family type, religious/spiritual identity, and appearance.
- Each person has the right to receive the information and support needed to move toward self-direction and self-development and affirmation within one's group identities, with special care being

given to students who have historically not received adequate educational services: students of color, low socioeconomic students, students with disabilities and students with nondominant language backgrounds.

- Each person has the right to understand the full magnitude and meaning of his or her educational choices and how those choices will affect future opportunities.
- Each person has the right to privacy and thereby the right to expect the counselor-student relationship to comply with all laws, policies, and ethical standards pertaining to confidentiality in the school setting.

In this document, ASCA specifies the principles of ethical behavior necessary to maintain the high standards of integrity, leadership, and professionalism among its members. The Ethical Standards for School Counselors were developed to clarify the nature of ethical responsibilities held in common by school counseling professionals. The purposes of this document are to:

- Serve as a guide for the ethical practices of all professional school counselors regardless of level, area, population served or membership in this professional association.
- Provide self-appraisal and peer evaluations regarding counselor responsibilities to students, parents/guardians, colleagues, and professional associates, schools, communities, and the counseling profession.
- Inform those served by the school counselor of acceptable counselor practices and expected professional behavior.

A.1. Responsibilities to Students

The professional school counselor:

a. Has a primary obligation to the student, who is to be treated with respect as a unique individual.

b. Is concerned with the educational, academic, career, personal, and social needs and encourages the maximum development of every student.

c. Respects the student's values and beliefs and does not impose the counselor's personal values.

d. Is knowledgeable of laws, regulations, and policies relating to students and strives to protect and inform students regarding their rights.

A.2. Confidentiality

The professional school counselor:

a. Informs students of the purposes, goals, techniques, and rules of procedure under which they may receive counseling at or before the time when the counseling relationship is entered. Disclosure notice includes the limits of confidentiality such as the possible necessity for consulting with other professionals, privileged communication, and legal or authoritative restraints. The meaning and limits of confidentiality are defined in developmentally appropriate terms to students.

b. Keeps information confidential unless disclosure is required to prevent clear and imminent danger to the student or others or when legal requirements demand that confidential information be revealed. Counselors will consult with appropriate professionals when in doubt as to the validity of an exception.

c. In absence of state legislation expressly forbidding disclosure, considers the ethical responsibility to provide information to an identified third party who, by his or her relationship with the student, is at a high risk of contracting a disease that is commonly known to be communicable and fatal. Disclosure requires satisfaction of all of the following conditions:

- Student identifies partner or the partner is highly identifiable.
- Counselor recommends the student notify partner and refrain from further high-risk behavior.
- Student refuses.
- Counselor informs the student of the intent to notify the partner.
- Counselor seeks legal consultation as to the legalities of informing the partner.

d. Requests of the court that disclosure not be required when the release of confidential information may potentially harm a student or the counseling relationship.

e. Protects the confidentiality of students' records and releases personal data in accordance with prescribed laws and school policies. Student information stored and transmitted electronically is treated with the same care as traditional student records.

f. Protects the confidentiality of information received in the counseling relationship as specified by federal and state laws, written policies, and applicable ethical standards. Such information is only to be revealed to others with the informed consent of the student, consistent with the counselor's ethical obligation.

g. Recognizes his or her primary obligation for confidentiality is to the student but balances that obligation with an understanding of the legal and inherent rights of parents/guardians to be the guiding voice in their children's lives.

A.3. Counseling Plans

The professional school counselor:

a. Provides students with a comprehensive school counseling program that includes a strong emphasis on working jointly with all students to develop academic and career goals.

b. Advocates for counseling plans supporting students' right to choose from the wide array of options when they leave secondary education. Such plans will be regularly reviewed to update students regarding critical information they need to make informed decisions.

A.4. Dual Relationships

The professional school counselor:

a. Avoids dual relationships that might impair his or her objectivity and increase the risk of harm to the student (e.g., counseling one's family members, close friends, or associates). If a dual relationship is unavoidable, the counselor is responsible for taking action to eliminate or reduce the potential for harm. Such safeguards might include informed consent, consultation, supervision, and documentation.

b. Avoids dual relationships with school personnel that might infringe on the integrity of the counselor/student relationship.

A.5. Appropriate Referrals

The professional school counselor:

a. Makes referrals when necessary or appropriate to outside resources. Appropriate referrals may necessitate informing both parents/guardians and students of applicable resources and making proper plans for transitions with minimal interruption of services. Students retain the right to discontinue the counseling relationship at any time.

A.6. Group Work

The professional school counselor:

a. Screens prospective group members and maintains an awareness of participants' needs and goals in relation to the goals of the group. The counselor takes reasonable precautions to protect members from physical and psychological harm resulting from interaction within the group.

b. Notifies parents/guardians and staff of group participation if the counselor deems it appropriate and if consistent with school board policy or practice.

c. Establishes clear expectations in the group setting and clearly states that confidentiality in group counseling cannot be guaranteed. Given the developmental and chronological ages of minors in schools, the counselor recognizes the tenuous nature of confidentiality for minors renders some topics inappropriate for group work in a school setting.

d. Follows up with group members and documents proceedings as appropriate.

A.7. Danger to Self or Others

The professional school counselor:

a. Informs parents/guardians or appropriate authorities when the student's condition indicates a clear and imminent danger to the student or others. This is to be done after careful deliberation and, where possible, after consultation with other counseling professionals.

b. Will attempt to minimize threat to a student and may choose to (1) inform the student of actions to be taken, (2) involve the student in a three-way communication with parents/guardians when breaching confidentiality, or (3) allow the student to have input as to how and to whom the breach will be made.

A.8. Student Records

The professional school counselor:

a. Maintains and secures records necessary for rendering professional services to the student as required by laws, regulations, institutional procedures, and confidentiality guidelines.

b. Keeps sole-possession records separate from students' educational records in keeping with state laws.

c. Recognizes the limits of sole-possession records and understands these records are a memory aid for the creator and in absence of privilege communication may be subpoenaed and may become educational records when they (1) are shared with others in verbal or written form, (2) include information other than professional opinion or personal observations, and/or (3) are made accessible to others.

d. Establishes a reasonable timeline for purging sole-possession records or case notes. Suggested guidelines include shredding sole-possession records when the student transitions to the next level, transfers to another school, or graduates. Careful discretion and deliberation should be applied before destroying sole-possession records that may be needed by a court of law such as notes on child abuse, suicide, sexual harassment, or violence.

A.9. Evaluation, Assessment, and Interpretation

The professional school counselor:

a. Adheres to all professional standards regarding selecting, administering, and interpreting assessment measures and only utilizes assessment measures that are within the scope of practice for school counselors.

b. Seeks specialized training regarding the use of electronically-based testing programs in administering, scoring, and interpreting that may differ from that required in more traditional assessments.

c. Considers confidentiality issues when utilizing evaluative or assessment instruments and electronically-based programs.

d. Provides interpretation of the nature, purposes, results, and potential impact of assessment/evaluation measures in language the student(s) can understand.

e. Monitors the use of assessment results and interpretations, and takes reasonable steps to prevent others from misusing the information.

f. Uses caution when utilizing assessment techniques, making evaluations, and interpreting the performance of populations not represented in the norm group on which an instrument is standardized.

g. Assesses the effectiveness of his or her program in having an impact on students' academic, career, and personal/social development through accountability measures especially examining efforts to close achievement, opportunity, and attainment gaps.

A.10. Technology

The professional school counselor:

a. Promotes the benefits of and clarifies the limitations of various appropriate technological applications. The counselor promotes technological applications (1) that are appropriate for the student's individual needs, (2) that the student understands how to use and (3) for which follow-up counseling assistance is provided.

b. Advocates for equal access to technology for all students, especially those historically underserved.

c. Takes appropriate and reasonable measures for maintaining confidentiality of student information and educational records stored or transmitted over electronic media including although not limited to fax, electronic mail, and instant messaging.

d. While working with students on a computer or similar technology, takes reasonable and appropriate measures to protect students from objectionable and/or harmful online material.

e. Who is engaged in the delivery of services involving technologies such as the telephone, videoconferencing, and the Internet takes responsible steps to protect students and others from harm.

A.11. Student Peer Support Program

The professional school counselor:

Has unique responsibilities when working with student-assistance programs. The school counselor is responsible for the welfare of students participating in peer-to-peer programs under his or her direction.

B. RESPONSIBILITIES TO PARENTS/GUARDIANS

B.1. Parent Rights and Responsibilities

The professional school counselor:

a. Respects the rights and responsibilities of parents/guardians for their children and endeavors to establish, as appropriate, a collaborative relationship with parents/guardians to facilitate the student's maximum development.

b. Adheres to laws, local guidelines, and ethical standards of practice when assisting parents/guardians experiencing family difficulties that interfere with the student's effectiveness and welfare.

c. Respects the confidentiality of parents/guardians.

d. Is sensitive to diversity among families and recognizes that all parents/guardians, custodial and noncustodial, are vested with certain rights and responsibilities for the welfare of their children by virtue of their role and according to law.

B.2. Parents/Guardians and Confidentiality

The professional school counselor:

a. Informs parents/guardians of the counselor's role with emphasis on the confidential nature of the counseling relationship between the counselor and student.

b. Recognizes that working with minors in a school setting may require counselors to collaborate with students' parents/guardians.

c. Provides parents/guardians with accurate, comprehensive, and relevant information in an objective and caring manner, as is appropriate and consistent with ethical responsibilities to the student.

d. Makes reasonable efforts to honor the wishes of parents/guardians concerning information regarding the student, and in cases of divorce or separation exercises a good-faith effort to keep both parents informed with regard to critical information with the exception of a court order.

C. RESPONSIBILITIES TO COLLEAGUES AND PROFESSIONAL ASSOCIATES

C.1. Professional Relationships

The professional school counselor:

a. Establishes and maintains professional relationships with faculty, staff, and administration to facilitate an optimum counseling program.

b. Treats colleagues with professional respect, courtesy, and fairness. The qualifications, views, and findings of colleagues are represented to accurately reflect the image of competent professionals.

c. Is aware of and utilizes related professionals, organizations, and other resources to whom the student may be referred.

C.2. Sharing Information With Other Professionals

The professional school counselor:

a. Promotes awareness and adherence to appropriate guidelines regarding confidentiality, the distinction between public and private information and staff consultation.

b. Provides professional personnel with accurate, objective, concise, and meaningful data necessary to adequately evaluate, counsel, and assist the student.

c. If a student is receiving services from another counselor or other mental health professional, the counselor, with student and/or parent/guardian consent, will inform the other professional and develop clear agreements to avoid confusion and conflict for the student.

d. Is knowledgeable about release of information and parental rights in sharing information.

D. RESPONSIBILITIES TO THE SCHOOL AND COMMUNITY

D.1. Responsibilities to the School

The professional school counselor:

a. Supports and protects the educational program against any infringement not in student's best interest.

b. Informs appropriate officials in accordance with school policy of conditions that may be potentially disruptive or damaging to the school's mission, personnel, and property while honoring the confidentiality between the student and counselor.

c. Is knowledgeable and supportive of the school's mission and connects his or her program to the school's mission.

d. Delineates and promotes the counselor's role and function in meeting the needs of those served. Counselors will notify appropriate officials of conditions that may limit or curtail their effectiveness in providing programs and services.

e. Accepts employment only for positions for which he or she is qualified by education, training, supervised experience, state and national professional credentials, and appropriate professional experience.

f. Advocates that administrators hire only qualified and competent individuals for professional counseling positions.

g. Assists in developing: (1) curricular and environmental conditions appropriate for the school and community, (2) educational procedures and programs to meet students' developmental needs and (3) a systematic evaluation process for comprehensive, developmental, standards-based school counseling programs, services, and personnel. The counselor is guided by the findings of the evaluation data in planning programs and services.

D.2. Responsibility to the Community

The professional school counselor:

a. Collaborates with agencies, organizations and individuals in the community in the best interest of students and without regard to personal reward or remuneration.

b. Extends his or her influence and opportunity to deliver a comprehensive school counseling program to all students by collaborating with community resources for student success.

E. RESPONSIBILITIES TO SELF

E.1. Professional Competence

The professional school counselor:

a. Functions within the boundaries of individual professional competence and accepts responsibility for the consequences of his or her actions.

b. Monitors personal well-being and effectiveness and does not participate in any activity that may lead to inadequate professional services or harm to a student.

c. Strives through personal initiative to maintain professional competence including technological literacy and to keep abreast of professional information. Professional and personal growth are ongoing throughout the counselor's career.

E.2. Diversity

The professional school counselor:

a. Affirms the diversity of students, staff, and families.

b. Expands and develops awareness of his or her own attitudes and beliefs affecting cultural values and biases and strives to attain cultural competence.

c. Possesses knowledge and understanding about how oppression, racism, discrimination, and stereotyping affects her or him personally and professionally.

d. Acquires educational, consultation, and training experiences to improve awareness, knowledge, skills, and effectiveness in working with diverse populations: ethnic/racial status, age, economic status, special needs, ESL or ELL, immigration status, sexual orientation, gender, gender identity/expression, family type, religious/spiritual identity, and appearance.

F. RESPONSIBILITIES TO THE PROFESSION

F.1. Professionalism

The professional school counselor:

a. Accepts the policies and procedures for handling ethical violations as a result of maintaining membership in the American School Counselor Association.

b. Conducts herself or himself in such a manner as to advance individual ethical practice and the profession.

c. Conducts appropriate research and reports findings in a manner consistent with acceptable educational and psychological research practices. The counselor advocates for the protection of the individual student's identity when using data for research or program planning.

d. Adheres to ethical standards of the profession, other official policy statements, such as ASCA's position statements, role statement, and the ASCA National Model, and relevant statutes established by federal, state and local governments, and when these are in conflict works responsibly for change.

e. Clearly distinguishes between statements and actions made as a private individual and those made as a representative of the school counseling profession.

f. Does not use his or her professional position to recruit or gain clients, consultees for his or her private practice or to seek and receive unjustified personal gains, unfair advantage, inappropriate relationships, or unearned goods or services.

F.2. Contribution to the Profession

The professional school counselor:

a. Actively participates in local, state, and national associations fostering the development and improvement of school counseling.

b. Contributes to the development of the profession through the sharing of skills, ideas, and expertise with colleagues.

c. Provides support and mentoring to novice professionals.

G. Maintenance of Standards

Ethical behavior among professional school counselors, association members and nonmembers, is expected at all times. When there exists serious doubt as to the ethical behavior of colleagues or if counselors are forced to work in situations or abide by policies that do not reflect the standards as outlined in these Ethical Standards for School Counselors, the counselor is obligated to take appropriate action to rectify the condition. The following procedure may serve as a guide:

1. The counselor should consult confidentially with a professional colleague to discuss the nature of a complaint to see if the professional colleague views the situation as an ethical violation.

2. When feasible, the counselor should directly approach the colleague whose behavior is in question to discuss the complaint and seek resolution.

3. If resolution is not forthcoming at the personal level, the counselor shall utilize the channels established within the school, school district, the state school counseling association, and ASCA's Ethics Committee.

4. If the matter still remains unresolved, referral for review and appropriate action should be made to the Ethics Committees in the following sequence:
   - state school counselor association
   - American School Counselor Association

5. The ASCA Ethics Committee is responsible for:
   - educating and consulting with the membership regarding ethical standards.
   - periodically reviewing and recommending changes in code.
   - receiving and processing questions to clarify the application of such standards; questions must be submitted in writing to the ASCA Ethics chair.
   - handling complaints of alleged violations of the ethical standards. At the national level, complaints should be submitted in writing to the ASCA Ethics Committee, c/o the Executive Director.

SOURCE: American School Counselor Association. Used with permission.

References

Bandura, A. (2001). Social cognitive theory: An agentic perspective. *Annual Review of Psychology, 52,* 1–26.

Chi, M. T. H., Feltovich, P. J., & Glaser, R. (1981). Categorization and representation of physics problems by experts and novices. *Cognitive Science, 5,* 121–152.

Culley, S., & Bond, T. (2004). *Integrative counselling skills in action* (2nd ed.). London: Sage.

De Jong, P., & Berg, I. K. (1998*). Interviewing for solutions.* Pacific Grove, CA: Brooks/Cole.

Dijkstra, J. A., van Wijck, R., Groothoff, J. W. (2006). The long-term lasting effectiveness on self-efficacy, attribution style, expression of emotions and quality of life of a body awareness program for chronic a-specific psychosomatic symptoms. *Patient Education & Counseling, 60* (1), 66–79.

Egan, G. (2002). *The skilled helper: A problem-management and opportunity-development approach to helping* (7th ed.). Belmont, CA: Wadsworth.

Ellerman, D. P. (2001). *Helping people help themselves: Autonomy-compatible assistance.* Policy Working Paper 2693. Washington, DC: World Bank.

Festinger, L. (1957). *A theory of cognitive dissonance.* Stanford, CA: Stanford University Press.

Groth-Marnat, G. (1997). *Handbook of psychological assessment* (3rd ed.). New York: Wiley.

Kazantzis, N., Deane, F. P., Ronan, K. R., & L'Abate, L. (2005). *Using homework assignments in cognitive behavior therapy.* New York: Routledge/Taylor & Francis.

Miller, W. R., & Rollnick, S. (2002). *Motivational interviewing: Preparing people to change.* New York: Guilford Press.

Miltenberger, R. G. (1997). *Behavior modification: Principles and procedures.* Pacific Grove, CA: Brooks/Cole.

Nelson, M. L., & Neufeldt, S. A. (1998). The pedagogy of counseling: A critical examination. *Counselor Education and Supervision, 38,* 70–88.

Norcross, J. C., Mrykalo, M. C., & Blagys, M. D. (2002). Auld Lang Syne: Success predictors, change processes, and self-reported outcomes of New Year's resolvers and nonresolvers. *Journal of Clinical Psychology, 58* (4), 397–405.

Pajares, F., & Urdan, T. (Eds.). (2006). *Adolescence and education, Vol. 5: Self-efficacy beliefs of adolescents.* Greenwich, CT: Information Age Publishing.

Parsons, R. D. (2008). *Counseling strategies that work: Evidence-based interventions for school counselors.* Boston: Allyn & Bacon.

Parsons, R. D. (2009a). *Thinking and acting like a behavioral school counselor.* Thousand Oaks, CA: Corwin.

Parsons, R. D. (2009b). *Thinking and acting like a cognitive school counselor.* Thousand Oaks, CA: Corwin.

Parsons, R. D. (2009c). *Thinking and acting like a solution-focused school counselor.* Thousand Oaks, CA: Corwin.

Patten, S., Vollman, A., & Thurston, W. (2000). The utility of the transtheoretical model of behavior change for HIV risk reduction in injection drug users. Retrieved December 11, 2008, from http://www.uwstout.edu/rs/2006/14Lenio.pdf

Pepinsky, H. B., & Pepinsky, P. (1954). *Counseling theory and practice.* New York: Ronald Press.

Prochaska, J. O., & DiClemente, C. C. (2002). Transtheoretical therapy. In F. W. Kaslow (Ed.), *Comprehensive handbook of psychotherapy: Integrative/eclectic: Vol. 4* (pp. 165–183). New York: Wiley.

Prochaska, J. O., DiClemente, C. C. & Norcross, J. C. (1992). In search of how people change: Applications to addictive behaviors. *American Psychologist, 47,* 1102–1114.

Prochaska, J. O., & Norcross, J. C. (1994). *Systems of psychotherapy: A transtheoretical analysis* (3rd ed.). Pacific Grove, CA: Brooks/Cole.

Prochaska, J. O., Redding, C. A., & Evers, K. (2002). The transtheoretical model and stages of change. In K. Glanz, B. K. Rimer, & F. M. Lewis (Eds.) *Health behavior and health education: Theory, research, and practice* (3rd ed.) (p. 26). San Francisco: Jossey-Bass.

Prochaska, J. O., & Velicer, W. F. (1997). The transtheoretical model of health behavior change. *American Journal of Health Promotion, 12,* 38–48.

Prochaska, J. O., Velicer, W. F., DiClemente, C. C., & Fava, J. (1988). Measuring processes of change: Applications to the cessation of smoking. *Journal of Consulting and Clinical Psychology, 56,* 520–528.

Reed, G. R., Velicer, W. F., Prochaska, J. O., Rossi J. S., Marcus, B. H. (1997). What makes a good staging algorithm: examples from regular exercise. *Am J Health Promotion, 12,* 57–66.

Scholl, R. (2002, September 15). The transtheoretical model of behavior change. Retrieved December 11, 2008, from http://www.cba.uri.edu/Scholl/Notes/TTM.html

Spencer, L. (2006). Applying the transtheoretical model to exercise: A systematic and comprehensive review of the literature. *Health Promotion Practice, 7* (4), 428–443.

Spiegler, M. D., & Guevremont, D. C. (2003). *Contemporary behavior therapy* (4th ed.). Pacific Grove, CA: Brooks/Cole.

Tillett, R. (1996). Psychotherapy assessment and treatment selection. *British Journal of Psychiatry, 168* (1), 10–15.

Tremmel, R. (1993). Zen and the art of reflective practice in teacher education. *Harvard Educational Review, 63* (4), 434–460.

Youngho, K. (2008). A staged-match intervention for exercise behavior changed based on the transtheoretical model. *Psychological Reports, 102* (3), 939–950.

Velicer, W. F., Prochaska, J. O., Fava, J. L., Norman, G. J., & Redding, C. (1998). Smoking cessation and stress management: Applications of the transtheoretical model of behavior change. *Homeostasis in Health and Disease, 38* (5–6), 216–233.

Index

CORWIN

A SAGE Company

The Corwin logo—a raven striding across an open book—represents the union of courage and learning. Corwin is committed to improving education for all learners by publishing books and other professional development resources for those serving the field of PreK–12 education. By providing practical, hands-on materials, Corwin continues to carry out the promise of its motto: **"Helping Educators Do Their Work Better."**